# THE MEAT
# YOU EAT

# THE MEAT YOU EAT

HOW CORPORATE
FARMING HAS
ENDANGERED
AMERICA'S
FOOD SUPPLY

## KEN MIDKIFF

ST. MARTIN'S GRIFFIN
NEW YORK

www.stmartins.com

Library of Congress Cataloging-in-Publication Data

Midkiff, Kenneth.
    The meat you eat : how corporate farming has endangered America's food supply / Ken Midkiff.
        p. cm.
    Includes bibliographical references (p. 181) and index (p. 215).
    ISBN 0-312-32535-5 (hc)
    ISBN 0-312-32536-3 (pbk)
    EAN 978-0-312-32536-7
    1. Meat industry and trade—Environmental aspects—United States.
2. Meat industry and trade—Health aspects—United States. 3. Meat industry and trade—Moral and ethical aspects—United States.
4. Agricultural industries—United States. I. Title.

HD9415.M53 2004
338.1'973—dc22                                        2004006098

10 9 8 7 6 5 4 3 2

# AUTHOR'S NOTE

Names appearing for the first time in quotes are pseudonyms. Readers should be aware that information contained on Web sites may have changed between when this book was written and when it is read.

# CONTENTS

# FOREWORD

WHEN I MUST EAT AWAY FROM HOME, I TRY TO FIND A restaurant that buys its meat from local farmers. Failing that, I eat fish and shellfish from the ocean, if available. Failing that, and for the purpose of survival only, I may resort to a vegetarian diet, though that is not my favorite way to survive. I am a livestock man and a meat eater, by liking and by conviction, but I dislike the products of the corporate meat industry and I avoid them whenever I can. My reasons are the ecological vandalism, the agricultural stupidity, the greed, the cruelty, and the nastiness of animal mass production.

Ken Midkiff lays it all out here in plain and readable English, and with blunt honesty. He writes with the assurance that he is speaking not only for himself but also for the increasingly numerous consumers and farmers who will know what he is talking about. These people understand with a growing anguish of conviction that we have done a fundamental wrong in allowing the agribusiness corporations to take over the stewardship of our farmland and our dinner tables, which rightly belongs to each one of us, and we have consented to the separation of food from goodness, kindness, health, gratitude, conviviality, and pleasure. These people see, in short, that we have given up to the agribusiness corporations a crucial part of our responsibility as human beings and that we now must think of ways to take it back.

The chapters that follow describe the apparently inalienable characteristics of the corporate meat industry. They tell of the abandonment of ecological and personal health as a standard of production, of the abuse of workers, of the exploitation of contract growers, of the close confinement and suffering of animals, of the destruction of small producers, of indifference to the welfare of neighbors, of pollution of land and water and air, of the generation of stench and messes, of contempt for the integrity of natural and human communities, of corruption by purchase of politicians and institutions, of the subversion of the public interest and its legal protections.

The point everywhere implicit in Ken Midkiff's book is that none of this ought to be surprising. All of it is merely the logical result of the decision to treat agriculture as an industry and creatures, including humans, as machines. When you impose on the living world and its living creatures a mechanical system that construes the will of its owners as the only operative will, and that understands live flesh only as matter or "raw material," then you have begun a process that cannot help but surround itself with an ever-expanding boundary of suffering and filth. Such a process is a disease that will degrade and finally destroy everything it affects.

The market for the food thus produced depends, obviously, on the ignorance of consumers. Knowledge therefore is dangerous to it, and this book is a much-needed bringer of knowledge. The more you know about this food, the less willing you will be to eat it.

But that is not all. The less willing you are to eat food of this kind, the more willing you will be to support the kinds of farming that produce better food. Good food, in fact, is possible. It comes from good farming, which also is possible. Ken Midkiff rightly ends his book by pointing the way to good farming and good food.

—Wendell Berry

# PREFACE

MOST PEOPLE IN THIS COUNTRY NOW KNOW WHAT A "downer cow" is (an animal sick and diseased to the point where she "stays down," because she can't rise to a standing position). I suspect that when I began to write this book, however, few knew that ground beef, steaks, roasts, and other beef cuts may have come from cows that could not stand on their own strength. Bovine spongiform encephalopy, BSE or "mad cow disease," was hardly a concern in this country. Those who followed international news were aware that an outbreak among livestock had occurred in England in the 1980s and that this had resulted in the slaughter and burning of a large number of cows and sheep. Although the British government originally denied that BSE could "jump" to humans, as of December 1, 2003, a total of 153 cases of the human version (variant of Cruezfeldt-Jakob Disease or vCJD) had been reported in the world: 143 from the United Kingdom, 6 from France, and 1 each from Canada, Ireland, Italy, and the United States (involving someone who had lived in the United Kingdom before moving to the United States). All of these cases were fatal, though for some reason that fact garnered little attention.

In May of 2003, the Canadian beef market collapsed due to the discovery of a single cow with BSE. The discovery led to the banning of beef imports from that country to most other nations, including the United States. Eventually, after many steps, principally involving the tracing of cattle and more intensive testing, were taken by the Canadian beef and slaughterhouse industry, the bans were partially removed and Canadian beef was again available for export throughout the world. No human illnesses have resulted to date from the Canadian incident; but the incubation period is measured in years and decades, so it could be that the human version of BSE—vCJD—will show up sometime between now and 2043.

That a downer cow in Washington State should be diagnosed as having BSE should come as no surprise to anyone acquainted with the industrial system of livestock production in this country, as this book will show. While it was not my original intent to explore the ramifications of BSE or vCJD, such was unavoidable after December 23, 2003—the date that the first case in this country was documented. The conclusion of this book, reached before the BSE documentation, is that the livestock-production industry in this country is so focused on profits that human health and safety are essentially ignored. The further discovery that humans may have been exposed to BSE confirms that conclusion.

In May of 2003—in other words, shortly after the Canadian incident—the U.S. Congress was presented with a legislative bill that would have prevented any products from downer cows from entering the human food system. A massive lobbying effort by the meat and dairy industry led to the defeat of that bill. Now, belatedly, USDA secretary Ann Venneman has directed that no downer cows should enter the market, particularly if the cow was "down" due to disease or illness.

To put it very bluntly, until December 23, 2003, the meat we ate came from both healthy and diseased cows. Government scientists and USDA officials, even the president, rushed to assure the meat-eating public that all was still well. The food supply, and beef in particular, was safe to eat. The media carried photos of Secretary Venneman, President Bush, and other officials chowing down on steaks and hamburgers. "An abundance of caution" had led to the ban of downer cows for slaughter, and the steps that were in place, we were told, protected the consuming public from contracting mad cow disease. The USDA and meatpacking industry officials stated that no potentially risky neural tissue had entered the food chain, that muscle and other meat tissue was not contaminated, and that therefore, once again, all was well.

This was not the case. As meatpacking workers pointed out, neural tissue had inadvertently become mixed in with ground meats. The mechanical extractor that removes meat from bones sometimes grinds up bone and neural tissue along with the meat. Scientists not associated with or paid by the meat industry stated that muscle tissue could in fact be responsible for transmitting the folded proteins, called prions, that cause mad cow disease (by making other proteins fold) and that other species susceptible to the disease, such as humans, would be placed at risk by eating this muscle tissue. Not only could muscle tissue itself be affected by the folded prions, but muscle tissue might also become contaminated with neural tissue during the slaughter and "disassembly"—the process by which meat is cut into parts. It can occur in a number of ways: from the stun bolt driving brain tissue back into the body of the animal to neural tissue being inadvertently mixed in with muscle tissue.

BSE is quite different from other diseases. First, its incubation period is extremely long. Once contracted by humans, the disease can take up to forty years for symptoms to develop. And once the symptoms (blindness, inability to talk, derangement, dementia, and "raving madness") appear, it is too late; death inevitably follows. Second, BSE is not caused by a germ or virus; the infectors are those mutated proteins. This is the only disease known that has such a source. A third difference involves BSE's effects: It causes the brain to become sponge-like, and at first the victim exhibits what seem to be psychiatric symptoms. The fourth difference is unusual but not unique: the disease "jumps" from species to species, on which it has different effects and goes by a different name, depending on the species. In affected sheep, for example, BSE is called scrapies, and a version that appears in deer and elk is called chronic wasting disease. (As far as is known, the latter is not transmissible to humans.)

More is unknown about BSE or vCJD than is known. Research has produced sometimes conflicting and contradictory discoveries and conclusions. For example, USDA scientists have insisted that transmission can only occur through eating neural tissue, as stated earlier, but it is telling that entire herds have been quarantined and even destroyed when one cow was found to have the disease. There is no doubt that eating neural tissue contaminated with folded proteins is a surefire way to contract the disease. Some scientists have also speculated that pesticides, and in particular those that use manganese as the active ingredient, may cause it. Manganese is a naturally occurring compound used in pesticides and in particular for insect control. However, most scientists still believe that the chance of contracting the disease remains very slim, due to its rarity.

The long incubation period is problematic. It was once a legal and common practice to convert whole dead animals to a feed additive through a rendering process with the results euphemistically called tankage. After the BSE scares in Europe, and after it was determined that the primary method of transmission was for ruminants (animals that have more than one stomach) to consume the neural tissue of other ruminants, in October of 1997, the USDA banned the addition of rendered ruminant parts in feed given to other ruminants. However, given that the incubation period for cows is at least four years and the incubation period for humans far longer, it is possible, indeed likely, that contaminated feeds were fed to cattle and that humans have eaten steaks, hamburgers, and other muscle tissue infected by the BSE prions. Only time will tell. Only one thing is beyond dispute: that by the time vCJD is recognized and diagnosed, it is too late.

There is a lesson to be learned here, one that forms the core of this book, and that is that in their zeal to maximize profits the livestock and meat industries (now virtually one and the same) have allowed unsafe and unhealthy products to be sold and consumed by an unsuspecting public. Self-monitoring is the rule in this country, and when it comes to meat inspection and industry regulation, the USDA has put the fox in charge of the henhouse.

# INTRODUCTION: GET BIG OR GET OUT

WILLIE NELSON CLIMBED ONTO THE MAKESHIFT STAGE, battered guitar in hand and trademark bandanna tied around his long and braided graying hair, before an expectant crowd of 3,000 farmers at the township meeting hall grounds. It was early April in northern Missouri, cold and blustery, a light covering of snow on the surrounding farmlands. Nelson was there to help raise funds for Lincoln Township, located in Putnam County, so that it could defend itself against a multimillion-dollar claim in a lawsuit being brought by Premium Standard Farms, Inc. Premium Standard, or PSF, is the second-largest producer of hogs in America. Nelson shielded his eyes and looked beyond the crowd to the western horizon, where row upon row of metal-sided buildings—each one housing thousands of hogs—gleamed in the dull afternoon sunlight. "It appears that the aliens have landed," he remarked offhandedly into the microphone.

However, these structures are not aliens but homegrown—the product of years of plans, schemes, and dreams on the part of people at the U.S. Department of Agriculture (USDA) and at the schools of agriculture at land-grant state universities, which have done the research and lobbied in the state legislatures and U.S. Congress to ensure that the "Get Big or Get Out" agricultural system pioneered by Ezra Taft Benson, Pres. Dwight Eisenhower's secretary of agriculture, became a reality. Since the 1950s, "Get Big or Get Out" has been the mantra repeated endlessly by agricultural economists.

The painter Grant Wood has only been dead for a bit over 60 years, but his classic work, *American Gothic,* is now hopelessly antiquated. The type of barn seen in the background of the painting, which depicts a farmer holding a pitchfork, his daughter at his side, has been replaced by all-purpose metal buildings. Rather than wood or cement floors, barns are built on grids with slats in the floor so that the excrement of thousands of hogs is flushed into a giant cesspit. These days it would be difficult to find a pitchfork on any corporate-owned farm. In fact, it would be difficult to find a hardworking farmer with a stiff-lipped, demure wife or daughter at his side. The total number of full-time farmers in this country amounts to less than 1 percent of the population (the exact figure according to the USDA in 2003 was .7 percent). At the turn of the last century, around 50 percent of Americans lived and worked on farms. In just over a century, we have transformed from a primarily rural to a primarily urban country.

What happened? How did the Jeffersonian notion of a pastoral nation—of people living off the land and selling the fruits of their labors—get turned upside down? We have become primarily a nation of urban and suburban consumers, dependent for our foods upon giant corporations that emphasize efficiency, uniformity, and consistency over all else.

Along I-70, I-35, and other interstate highways in Kansas, signs have been erected by the Kansas Farm Bureau that proudly proclaim: ONE KANSAS FARMER FEEDS 129 PEOPLE, PLUS YOU. That means 130 people are dependent for their sustenance upon *one* Kansas farmer. Chances are good that this one Kansas farmer raises only one crop or one type of livestock. Wheat is the primary crop in western Kansas, and wheat does supply our daily bread. The second and third crops, however—soybeans and corn—are grown to the exclusion of almost everything else in central and eastern Kansas. These crops don't feed you and me; they go right to the pigs.

Directly or indirectly, the food every Kansas farmer produces is the result of "monoculture," a concept an older generation might have tagged "putting all of your eggs in one basket." Monoculture is what has led to the decline, even the demise, of the American farmer. Monoculture is the direct result of the "Get Big or Get Out" philosophy adopted after World War II, aided and abetted by the USDA, land-grant colleges and universities, and county extension agents. To get big, farmers borrowed against their lands and mortgaged the farms, so that they could acquire more land and bigger machinery. Then they took out other loans to pay for the fuel, seeds, pesticides, and chemical fertilizers necessitated by having more land and using bigger machinery.

When farmers couldn't pay their loans, due to crop failure or low prices and exacerbated by the farm crisis of the mid-1980s, when land values plummeted, farmers lost their lands.

Larger and larger farmers, or investors who had absolutely no intention of ever setting foot on the farm, acquired these lands, sometimes on the courthouse steps. A cursory look at county plat maps will reveal that in many states land ownership is heavily dominated by businesses that are incorporated as "Land Trust, Inc."

Today the average size of a farm in America is 500 acres, up from 120 acres in 1900. As farms became larger and larger and machinery replaced farmworkers, the number of people making their living from the land declined. Farmers moved to area towns or to distant cities. The sons and daughters of former farmers were disenfranchised. Inheritance taxes, land prices, and the enticements offered by agribusiness companies to students at colleges and universities with schools of agriculture all combined to ensure that they weren't kept "down on the farm."

In his seminal book *The Unsettling of America,* Wendell Berry makes a distinction between "agriculture" and "agribusiness," the first denoting the culture of rural life and the second the incorporation of rural life. The battle now defines this country, as large corporations have come to own more and more of America's farmlands and are attempting to control the entire production of certain farm animals and their products. The aliens have indeed landed.

This book will detail why what we eat is both unsafe and unhealthy. We gamble with our health and maybe even our life every time we purchase meat, milk, or eggs in a supermarket and every time we order a burger at a fast-food restaurant. I will reveal in detail how the animals that provide us with meat, milk, and eggs are raised in this country and how we have turned over what we eat to large corporations that are more concerned about profit than about health, safety, taste, humane treatment of animals, land stewardship, or the quality of rural life. In the process, we have made ourselves, our economy, and our very food supply extremely vulnerable, as the recent outbreak of BSE has revealed.

There is plenty of blame to go around, but the monoculture system is a good place to start, for it affects not just crops but also animals. Today, for example, there are only three commercial breeds of hogs, one of broiler chickens, one of dairy cattle, one of salmon, and two of beef. Genetic similarity makes these mono-breeds extremely susceptible to disease. (In fact, in the large confined feeding operations in which the animals are kept, it has become necessary for workers and visitors to "shower in"—put on sanitized coverings to protect the animals in the enclosed facilities from pathogens.) Diversity is always to be desired, whether stock investments or livestock are at issue. The more baskets we can put our eggs in, the better off we are. Yet the livestock industries have been moving in the opposite direction. Livestock production has not only been concentrated in larger and larger operations, but these facilities also are located in small areas of the country. Circle Four, so called because it was originally developed by four agribusiness corporations and located near Milford, Utah, raises over a million hogs inside a few square miles. The Central Valley of California is glutted with gigantic dairies. Greeley, Colorado, has enclosures housing millions of beef steers in a feedlot connected to a slaughterhouse. In the Panhandle areas of Texas and Oklahoma are giant feedlots with millions of steers. In southwest Missouri's McDonald County, 13 million chickens are housed on any given day. The same holds true for North Georgia, the DelMarVa area of Chesapeake Bay in Maryland, northwest Arkansas, and northeast Oklahoma. Millions of commercially raised Atlantic salmon are now contained in pens in the Georgia Strait of British Columbia.

This concentration of our food supply is also a national security threat. A few dedicated terrorists with a crude map could, in a few days, wipe out most of the food supply of this country. We were much less vulnerable when farm animals were dispersed all over the country. Instead of slaughterhouses in every small town, there are now a very few slaughterhouses that are responsible for supplying almost all the meats in this country. Instead of every farm containing a few hens, there are a few egg-laying facilities that provide 90 percent of this country's supply of eggs, and the dairy industry continues to convert to larger and larger herd sizes. In northern Missouri one hog company is responsible for producing 2,500,000 hogs per year in a three-county area; in Utah one company is responsible for producing 1 million hogs per year in one valley.

Old MacDonald, the one who had a farm, not the one developed by Ray Kroc, would not recognize any of these operations as "farms." And, indeed, the industrial model we now associate with Kroc's enterprises has been applied to livestock production facilities. The giant companies own it all, from feed mills, to nurseries, to finishing operations, to slaughterhouses, to delivery, to retailers. An Illinois farmer phrased it so memorably: "They control it from semen to cellophane." Their goal is uniformity of product, the better to maximize volume, efficiency, and the speed of the so-called disassembly line, where the cadavers are carved up. The products that land on the store shelves are dismally uniform; every pork chop looks and tastes like every other pork chop. What they also have in common is that the animal from which they have been taken has been raised on a diet of antibiotics. As a result, the meat is now laden with pathogens—disease-causing bacteria—that have grown resistant to those antibiotics, as well as with heavy metals used as appetite enhancers. No wonder the meat tastes lousy.

We have placed our trust in industries run by people who own and manage the feed mills, the fish nurseries, the finishing houses, the laying houses, and the slaughterhouses but who live nowhere near what they raise. Their products are not sold locally; they are shipped hundreds or even thousands of miles for value-added processing. While the products may eventually end up back in the small-town supermarket or at the local McDonald's, the journey, however long it has been, has transformed the meat, milk, and eggs into yet more units of production.

Although modern livestock facilities are clearly based on an industrial model, in the eyes of state and federal agencies they fit the legal description of "farm." This suits the owners and managers of these operations just fine, because it allows them generous tax breaks and exemptions from a number of environmental laws. Attempts by state legislators, such as Rep. Chuck Graham of Missouri, to introduce language that would change the classification of industrial livestock operations from "agriculture" to "industry" have been met by overwhelming resistance and have failed.

What most of us think of as farming barely exists. There are fewer and fewer individual farmers tilling their own soil. Fewer farm kids are playing in the creek, which has in any case most likely been poisoned with fertilizer, pesticides, or bacteria. Farmwives no longer are baking pies and setting them on window ledges to cool. There are fewer cows lowing in the green pastures, hogs wallowing in the muck of their pens, or roosters crowing at dawn. The owners and CEOs of today's agribusiness operations live in New York City, Chicago, or Dallas–Fort Worth. Joe Luter, the CEO of Smithfield Foods, the largest producer of pork in the world, describes his occupation as "farmer" yet lives in a condo on Park Avenue in New York City. Members of Congress are the major investors. These "farmers" hire migrant workers to do the hard work of producing millions of steers, hogs, and broilers and filling our supermarkets with billions of cartons of eggs and milk.

This is not culture and it is not agriculture; it is not even the business of farming. It is agribusiness. Managers and corporate CEOs are not farmers. These executives care about the profit margin, not about the health and safety of the meat, milk, and eggs. American Gothic has become Gothic Horror.

## Down on the Corporate Farm

Looking down at the discolored water flowing under the low bridge, Jean sighed. "When I was a kid—not all that long ago, you know—we used to jump off this bridge and go swimming right down there. Not anymore. I don't even like to look at it. It doesn't even smell good—smells like wet chickens." Jean was, in her words, "bred, born, and raised here." Now she is a teacher at the local prison, and with her graying hair tucked into a bun and her shapeless dresses she looks the part of a schoolmarm. But looks can deceive. Jean knows animals, both as a self-professed "farm girl" and as a graduate of the Texas Agriculture and Mining University in Bryan–College Station, where she got a doctoral degree in animal science. She writes frequently about the ills of corporate agriculture and, in particular, what it has done to her area.

There is a popular song that begins, "The stars at night are big and bright deep in the heart of Texas." Those lyrics apply poorly to the Navasota River region of East Central Texas. The 8 million broiler chickens owned by Sanderson Farms, one of the largest poultry companies in the world, confined in contract operations in the watershed, don't see the sky at all, much less the stars. The Navasota River is contaminated with chicken wastes. No one denies this, since the contract growers (see later) for Sanderson Farms have been spreading the litter from the chicken houses on the fields adjacent to the confinement buildings for the past ten years. Containing chicken excrement and some "feed additives," the litter is removed from the growing houses between changes in flocks, which occur about every seven weeks. Millions of pounds of chicken excrement get applied to the same fields year after year. In 1997, Sanderson Farms was ranked by the Environmental Protection Agency as the twenty-fourth-largest polluter in the country; it released over 2 million (2,195,343 to be exact) pounds of toxic wastes to the waters of the company's home state of Mississippi. Having fouled the home waters, the company is now doing the same to the water in central Texas.

The chicken litter that contains this waste is normally not sent directly into streams and rivers; rather, it is dumped on adjacent farm fields—as fertilizer, allegedly. However, applied to the same areas year after year, the waste eventually builds up and runs off into small tributary streams of the area—or directly into the Navasota. The river contains about every conceivable pollutant: giardia, assorted pathogens, nitrates, phosphorous, arsenic, selenium, and what are termed suspended solids. This might make a fine—although somewhat toxic—stew, but it makes a lousy habitat for fish, and an even worse place to swim.

Given that the Navasota River doesn't even come close to meeting the water quality standards outlined in the federal Clean Water Act, which specifies that every water body must be both fishable and swimmable, it has been placed on the "impaired water body" list, sometimes called the 303(d) list (referring to Section 303[d] of the federal Clean Water Act). In EPA bureaucratese, this means it is unfit for "whole body contact recreation." In plain English, this means that swimming and wading here are hazardous to health. The Navasota River became so polluted that in 2002 the Brazos River Authority, a quasi-governmental agency responsible for water quality in the Brazos River watershed (the Navasota is a tributary to the Brazos), applied for and received a $502,000 grant from the USDA. Everyone knew that the focus of the grant was to assist Sanderson's contract growers in cleaning up the mess they made and to help them devise ways to keep chicken crap out of the water. Conveniently, several of those responsible for drafting and obtaining the grant were employed by or associated with Sanderson Farms and also sat on a subcommittee of the Brazos River Authority. The company was, of course, delighted to receive taxpayer assistance to restore and protect the Navasota.

It was pointed out at Brazos River Authority meetings that the monies provided were specifically prohibited from being given to Concentrated Animal Feeding Operations, or CAFOs, which is what Sanderson is. The funds were authorized by the Congress as part of the Environmental Quality Improvement Program (EQIP), and the USDA, under considerable pressure, prohibited any of the funds from going to "large CAFOs"—defined as companies with over 1,000 animal units (100,000 chickens). The Natural Resource Conservation Service (NRCS, the grant-making wing of the USDA) explained that the monies were being given to the Brazos River Authority and therefore only indirectly to contract growers. No money, they explained, was going to Sanderson. But the fact remains that Sanderson Farms owns all the chickens whose wastes are being dumped onto the land in such quantities that it produces runoff into local streams and rivers.

Rather than forcing Sanderson to prevent such waste from entering the waters, the USDA sent bucketloads of cash to contract growers for Sanderson. Contract growers, as we shall see, are little more than serfs, having signed away their land for the privilege of raising Sanderson's chickens for less than minimum wage. The growers don't meet any criterion of "contractor" as defined by the Internal Revenue Service, but the Brazos River Authority could use them to direct funds to benefit Sanderson while claiming the money was going to these contractors.

What about the Navasota River? Recent water-quality monitoring tests show that nothing has really improved. Some argue that it is worse in some ways. Most of the EQIP funds were used by the growers to construct composters or manure storage sheds, structures that merely house wastes for later dumping. Sooner or later, in one form or another, the wastes were dumped, and the river got more polluted.

For millennia, manure has been applied as fertilizer to crops that required much nitrogen, such as corn and other grasslike plants. On the one hand, once upon a time, crops were rotated through a cycle, dictating that a legume (soybeans, alfalfa) that "fixed" nitrogen in the soil, by removing it from the air and transporting it to the plant's roots, preceded corn or wheat, which need lots of nitrogen. Other years, the fields were devoted to pasture or lay fallow. Typically, manure from farm animals was applied one of every five years. Large commercial livestock operations, on the other hand, use fixed irrigation systems or other methods that require manure to be applied to the same fields year after year. This is contrary to every principle learned by farmers over the years. Animal manure has always proved a cheap and highly effective fertilizer, but it was often in short supply, given that most farmers didn't raise huge numbers of animals. Farmers were careful not to overapply manure; that was simply wasting a valuable resource. Today's giant livestock operations don't view manure as fertilizer but as a waste product, and they deal with it as a waste disposal problem akin to a toxic waste—which, in the volume it gets produced, it is. Agribusinesses may tout the value of manure as fertilizer, but they don't really treat it as such. They're really just looking for ways to get rid of it. Agribusinesses don't make money from proper manure handling; they make money by controlling markets and selling meat, milk, and eggs.

This, then, is the source of all the environmental problems associated with agribusiness: too much manure in one place.

As one farmer put it, "Mother Nature never intended for eighty-thousand hogs to shit in the same spot." The EPA acknowledges that pollution from agribusiness operation poses the single largest threat to this country's waters. Thousands of miles of streams and rivers, and many hundreds of lakes, are contaminated with "nutrients from livestock operations," as they put it euphemistically. Too much shit in the same spot.

What have federal and state environmental protection agencies done about this problem, which now exists across America? In a word: nothing. Water-quality monitoring and testing by state and federal officials, as well as by trained and certified volunteers, have documented the contamination, but very few state, and no federal, agencies are willing to take on an industry with as much clout as agribusiness. As was the case with the Brazos River Authority, government's approach is to throw money at the problem. However, the ones responsible for the pollution in the first place are the ones who receive the money. The incentive is therefore not to clean up but to pollute more.

For years, the owners and managers of CAFOs and the state and federal agencies had been claiming in the face of mounting studies that there was no evidence that their operations were producing high and unhealthy levels of toxic air emissions, particularly hydrogen sulfide. Toxic air emission, sometimes called hazardous air pollutant, or HAP, is defined in the Clean Air Act and its regulations as an air contaminant that causes immediate or long-term negative impacts on human health. High levels of hydrogen sulfide have a deadly effect; long-term exposure at lower levels can cause a variety of ills, particularly to children. When monitoring around large hog and poultry operations sponsored by the EPA found that off-site levels of various air contaminants were in violation of the National Ambient Air Quality Standards and a study by the National Research Council documented the dangerous emission levels, the EPA found itself with a problem that it could not ignore.

The EPA's response was to propose to give "safe harbor" to the largest—and most violative—CAFOs. In exchange for the CAFOs' allowing the EPA to conduct air monitoring in and around these facilities, the agency would agree not to use any of the data in enforcement actions. This suggested deal was unprecedented. The federal agency mandated with the authority, indeed the requirement, to protect the environment of this country would grant amnesty to the offenders and, worse, coordinate and cooperate with them. It was suggested that the motto of the EPA should be changed to "Protecting Polluters, Not the Environment." Fortunately, word of this deal leaked out and the national news agencies jumped on the story. The EPA agreed to meet with representatives of sustainable agriculture, conservation, and environmental organizations but would not agree to halt adoption of the deal. This exposure did manage to slow down this "safe harbor" notion. As of this writing, no such policy is in place. However, since 2001 no CAFO has been cited by the EPA for violating the Clean Air Act.

The U.S. House and Senate have been even less inclined to pressure the agencies to enforce the Clean Water Act and Clean Air Act than the agencies have been to take any action. In fact, the U.S. Congress has generally leaned toward assisting the large CAFOs, even when urged to take action by constituents. Rural residents and small, independent farmers have little or no political clout. In addition, the areas in which the agribusiness corporations have located their operations are not very politically important, due to declining populations and more important voting blocks in large metropolitan areas. Not so with the offices of agribusiness and commodity organizations. With their newsletters, alert systems, and political savvy, they can swing a large number of votes. Their headquarters are also in large cities, where they garner favorable treatment from regional and national media. National politicians know this and respond to those organizations' wishes. Consequently, there has been no serious attempt in either the U.S. House or Senate to rein in the large agribusiness companies. To the contrary, the inclination of U.S. representatives and senators has been to accede to the companies' demands and to provide "solutions" for their problems.

The same situation exists in most state capitols. While state representatives must give some attention to their constituents, what state legislators do is generally unknown in their district. State houses are more apt to take voice, not "roll call," votes. Even when roll calls are taken, this information typically is not reported in local newspapers. Public oversight is not a concern of state politicians, at least not on farm or rural issues.

County commissions, however, have been responsive to the concerns of residents. A number of counties from South Carolina to Utah have banned CAFOs or placed severe restrictions on their locations, often requiring setbacks of many thousands of feet from occupied dwellings, public facilities, churches, and recreational areas. However, in a series of bills introduced in state houses across the nation, in what appears to have been a coordinated effort, there were attempts to prohibit the counties from taking such actions. Fortunately, county associations across the country opposed these bills, and most were defeated. In Iowa, a legal contest has developed in Worth County, which placed several restrictions on CAFOs. The Farm Bureau challenged this action in court, and the county, along with the Iowa Farmers' Union, the Worth County Concerned Citizens, and the Sierra Club, filed counterclaims asserting the right, the duty, of the Worth County Commission to pass such ordinances.

For neighbors of the large poultry operations, odor, flies, and poultry dust containing dander and disease are constant problems. In fact, stench and flies cause the most complaints. These complaints don't come, as the livestock companies claim and would have everyone believe, from urban "move-ins." Rather, they tend to come from longtime residents—from folks who are familiar with the smells associated with rural life. Given that the population shift in this country over the past several decades has been from rural areas to towns and cities, not the other way around, those who live in the country tend to be people who have chosen to stick it out on their farms, not newcomers.

"It doesn't smell like money to me; it just flat stinks" is a common enough statement by those who live next to the large hog, dairy, beef, and poultry operations. Some live in houses literally blackened with the flies that breed in the litter and waste. Simple pleasures once associated with farming and country life, such as sitting on the front porch with a cup of coffee and a slice of pie, are no longer possible.

Farmers and other rural residents have been mystified by

the failure of the traditional farm organizations to provide any opposition to the takeover of agriculture by Big Business. What has been even more perplexing is that the traditional farm organizations have frequently sided with the agribusiness corporations, taking positions detrimental to their own members. The farm organizations have even filed suit against laws and ordinances designed to protect farmers and rural residents, as in Worth County, Iowa. That the Farm Bureau Federation would take such positions in favor of Big Ag is not at all surprising considering it owns a large number of shares in agribusiness corporations, for example, 18,672 shares of Premium Standard Farms, Inc. The Farm Bureau has also been, for years, a right-wing organization, supportive of an economic system that rewards the rich and penalizes the poor. And, finally, it must be remembered that the Farm Bureau makes most of its money selling insurance and requires all policyholders to become members of the Farm Bureau Federation. A large number of city dwellers are policyholders and don't even realize that the Farm Bureau is lobbying in D.C. and the state capitals or has filed lawsuits contrary to the interests of real farmers.

However, none of the above except perhaps the conservative tendency applies to such organizations as the Cattlemen's Beef Association, the Corn Growers, Soybean Growers, and other traditional agricultural interest groups. While occasionally a connective interest is revealed, such as the Corn Growers' supporting hog CAFOs because these operations buy lots of grain, there is no such justification for the Soybean or Rice Growers. It can only be assumed that there is some sort of leftover adherence to the "domino theory": today hogs—tomorrow soybeans.

Some of these organizations have raised the specter of the federal government treading upon sacred "private property rights," but many of the lawsuits filed to date make the opposite claim: Corporations are intruding upon the property rights of neighbors, up to and including driving down property values. Devaluation of property around CAFOs is well documented; residences near a CAFO are nearly impossible to sell. In addition, some tax assessors have ruled that lands adjacent to a CAFO are worth 30 percent less than they were before the CAFO was there. In any event, the commodity groups have staunchly opposed any attempt, even the very feeble ones, by state and federal agencies or elected officials to impose restrictions or bring enforcement actions on large companies that are running the members of these organizations out of business.

The only help so far has been provided by the courts. Citizens have filed and won nuisance suits, claiming harm to their persons or property from odor, flies, fouled wells, polluted streams, and decreased property values. Naturally, agribusiness bemoans this "litigious society," but when government agencies are part of the problem, attorneys and judges are literally the court of last resort. But the courts can act only after some injurious or illegal act has occurred; consequently, citizens must sit back and wait for an agribusiness corporation to violate a law. Unfortunately, the courts generally only react; prevention is not something that the judicial system would typically enforce. While the compliance record of large industrial-strength livestock operations is horrible, the courts have been generous in awarding monetary damages to plaintiff-citizens but have been reluctant to order closure of the offending operation. A county judge in rural Alabama, while ordering a CAFO to stop stinking up the neighborhood, noted that the plaintiffs were a group of hardworking longtime residents who only asked that they be treated as they would treat others. Like most other plaintiffs in these cases, they had lived in the area for generations and knew the smell of farming operations; but they had never smelled anything like this. The Wooten brothers, who were operating under a contract with Gold Kist, Inc., obtained a grant in the amount of $219,000 from the USDA/NRCS to install aeration devices in their cesspit, and the judge reluctantly agreed to let the facility be restocked with hogs. According to one of the nearby residents, it stinks just as bad as before.

### What Magic Valley?

Len Miracle crested the hill in his new car and then screeched to a halt. Filling a low spot in the road ahead and coursing down a ditch on the lower side was liquefied cow crap. Len already didn't like the large dairies that had moved into his neighborhood, west of Twin Falls, Idaho, and just a bit south of Buhl. Here was just one more reason. The stink from the dairy just south of his house was enough to gag a maggot, he told anyone who would listen. "And look," he would add to a visitor to his house. "Out here under the cottonwood tree, I've got this big fruit jar rigged up as a fly trap. The damned thing fills up every day."

Len's is a tale of woe. How he came back to live out his life, after retiring from years as an editor of a popular outdoor magazine, in the Snake River Plains, in the Magic Valley (an area made fertile through irrigation). This was where he was born and grew up, before the bright lights of New York tugged him away. Len soon learned that he couldn't quite come home again. Shortly after he had bought a small house and he and his wife moved in, he was out in the garage one morning, readying his fly-fishing gear for a try at the trout in Salmon Valley Creek just off to the west, when he noticed heavy machinery and concrete trucks moving south. By the time he got back from his trip ("Caught some fine trout," he recalls), a large "pond"—later he found it was actually a cesspit—had been dug and a concrete pad had been poured. Within a couple of months, Len and his wife had become reluctant neighbors to a large dairy. This was not any ordinary dairy; the number of cows was in the thousands. When he went around to talk things over with his neighbors, he found that they had the same problems and concerns he did: stink and flies. Some had filed complaints with the Idaho State Department of Agriculture as individuals, not as part of an organized group. The ISDA sent out some inspectors and they sniffed around (literally). In an eventual hearing it was ruled that the dairy was producing "normal agricultural odors."

Miracle is a large, rawboned man and certainly not shy or reticent. "Normal agricultural odors, my ass!" he bellowed at the meeting before the Twin Falls County commissioners. "There's nothing 'normal' about this. It's going to run us all out of the county!" Farmer after farmer got up to echo the same concerns; they all farmed and they understood that animal excrement doesn't smell good, but the large dairies were producing manure in such volume that the reek was overwhelming. Some complained of gagging, vomiting, asthma attacks. The stench of cow manure and rotting carcasses had ruined their life. The commissioners finally conceded that something needed to be done, because they were being deluged with complaints. They did what government officials do everywhere: appointed a working group and gave its members instructions to report back.

In due time, the report came back. The group, which included dairy owners, environmentalists, and rural residents, deadlocked when it came to making recommendations. They had devised a "matrix"—a chart indicating the various factors for approving or disapproving of locations for large dairies. But the group could not reach agreement about the odor problem. The Idaho Dairy Association was well organized and politically powerful. Any attempt to regulate the industry met with successful resistance. Meanwhile, liquefied manure was running off fields, down and across roads, into the trout streams, and eventually making its way into the Snake River. Most rural residents used private drinking water wells, and when one well tested high for nitrates, several others got their waters tested. Soon drinking bottled water became routine for farmers who had once enjoyed cold drafts of water from their wells.

Similar tales come from anyplace large confinement operations have been constructed. The species of animal doesn't matter—hogs in North Carolina, Iowa, or the Texas Panhandle, broiler chickens in Ohio or Arkansas or Oklahoma, or dairy herds in Erath County, Texas, Curry County, New Mexico, or Kern County, California. The fouling of the air, water, and land is the same. With salmon-producing aquabusinesses springing up, such as those located off the coast of British Columbia, the ocean may now be added to this list of polluted places.

Apologists for the meat industries claim that pollution is simply a result of inept management. The fact is, however, that sheer size makes confinement operations unmanageable. Manure runoff occurs at small farms; any time manure is applied, even as true fertilizer, rainfall can cause some of it to be carried off the land and into a nearby creek. But there is simply no comparison between the runoff produced by a few head of livestock and the runoff produced by tens of thousands of animals. Manure from a few animals might taint local creeks; manure from thousands of animals will transform those creeks into sewers. Some facilities are managed better than others; it is possible to keep down stink and clouds of flies. However, even the best-managed operations cannot make 5,000 cows or 80,000 hogs or 2 million chickens smell like anything other than what they are.

Some companies claim to have found a solution, usually involving some type of chemical or bacteria digester. None of these magic solutions have been subjected to objective testing that might prove whether they actually do what it is claimed they do. Even if these did work and even if the odor were reduced by half (which none claim), the odor from 80,000 hogs would smell like, well, that from 40,000 hogs. Not much of a solution there.

The only real solution to fouling the air, land, and water is to downsize, to return to smaller farms. Diversified farms and independent family farmers can feed America. They did so for years, right up to the time when the large corporations began their push for market control of agriculture, and with minimal pollution and negative impact on their neighbors. The "vertical integration" so prized by agribusiness corporations simply means controlling everything from feed mills to retail delivery, from squeal to meal—again, from semen to cellophane.

Proponents of Bigger Is Better will proudly claim that mammoth hog, chicken, beef, and dairy operations are all about "feeding a hungry nation and world." But even a cursory glance back to the days before agribusiness will reveal that there has never been a shortage of meat, milk, or eggs in this country. To the contrary, small farmers were doing a fine job of keeping everyone fed. Domestic consumption of pork, for example, has remained constant over the past thirty years, at about 90 million hogs per year. Though the population of this country has risen exponentially, the per-capita consumption of the "other white meat" has decreased and consequently domestic demand has remained about the same. It is true that more hogs are raised in North Carolina today than in 1975, but this is primarily due to the ambitions of Wendell Murphy (the "Boss Hog," according to a series of Pulitzer-winning articles about him in the *Charlotte Observer*), who, before selling out to Smithfield, contracted with hundreds of farmers to raise hogs. As a member of the North Carolina State Senate, he was also instrumental in getting a number of bills passed that benefited the hog-raising industry. North Carolina is now giving Iowa a run for its money as the number-one state in producing hogs. But in other states, even in the traditional "corn and hogs" midwestern states, the number of hogs raised has either remained about the same as the mid-1970s or actually declined. There were 5 million more hogs produced in Missouri in 1975 than in the most recent year.

What *has* changed dramatically is the number of growers. In the United States today, there are almost no independent producers of hogs or chickens. As I will show in the chapters on these species, a few companies control it all. Dairy herds, while less subject to corporate ownership, are increasing rapidly in size in response to government programs that encourage them to do so.

One source of the drive for size, as I suggested earlier, is the many colleges of agriculture at land-grant universities that now have "commercial agriculture" divisions whose faculty and facilities are funded by, naturally, large corporations. In essence, these departments act as the research and development arms for agribusinesses. They have developed chickens with large breasts and legs to respond to "market demand" (never mind that the poor creatures can barely walk), strains of hogs that have a high feed-to-market weight ratio, and systems of animal science and care that focus almost solely upon profits. In short, the system of private commercial livestock production has largely been researched and developed by public universities with grant funding from agribusiness corporations. Instead of working for the public good, these commercial agriculture "biostitutes," full of scientists for hire, have developed a system of agriculture that fouls the air and water, runs family farmers off the land, benefits corporate benefactors, and provides unsafe and unhealthy foods to the consuming public. Some family farmers don't mince words about these university researchers and just call them whores.

The system that has been developed has nothing whatsoever to do with "feeding a hungry world," but it does have everything to do with filling the pockets of greedy industrialists. While his (there are as yet no women running agribusinesses) personal interests are his own, the top-ranking executives of an agribusiness could care less about whether or not a starving child in Calcutta is fed. The CEO's concern is how well his company is doing in the Dow Jones projections for the next quarter and whether this quarter met previous projections. This is neither right nor wrong; it is a simple fact. That executive is not paid to feed starving people; he is paid to run a profitable company. If his product reaches Calcutta, that is incidental, not intentional.

Corporations are about money. In his book *In the Absence of the Sacred,* Jerry Mander recounts what we should know about corporations, and the first principle is that they exist to make money. Everything else is secondary, tertiary, or even nonexistent. Corporations care about people only to the extent that people are consumers of the corporate product. Mander also points out that corporations have no morals. They are neither moral nor immoral but amoral—lacking morals altogether. Feeding a hungry world? That is only a justification for fouling the air and water. Running family farmers out of business; ruining the economies of small towns; destroying the rural quality of life; mangling, dismembering, and maiming employees; producing foods that are unsafe and unhealthy? When confronted with some unintended consequences of the industrial mode of production of meat, milk, and eggs, the corporate spokesman hauls out things like the following from his bag of tricks: "It is unfortunate, but it must be kept in mind that this is the way things must be done if we're going to feed the world."

Feeding a hungry world has become an integral part of

agribusiness-speak, and it is nothing less than the Big Lie. The takeover of food production by corporate agribusiness has done nothing to relieve the fact that there are still people starving in Nigeria, Bangladesh, and even North, Central, and South America. Some would insist that the so-called Green Revolution, the exportation of agricultural methods, seeds, and species developed in this country to the Third World, has merely resulted in the destruction of indigenous systems and methods that had fed native peoples for millennia. Vandiva Shiva, a rural economist from India, believes that the Green Revolution has led to a deepening shortage of foods in her country by introducing a type of agriculture totally unsuited to India—and in the process has displaced sustainable farmers. Agribusiness has everything to do with market control and nothing to do with producing safe and healthy foods (and less than nothing to do with feeding the world).

Agribusinesses raise animals purely with human consumption in mind. Sheep, cows, goats, hogs, and chickens are "units of production" destined for the market; their lives are as short as they can be. Dairy cows and laying hens live a bit longer, as they are valued for their milk and eggs. But when ole Bessie's milk production tapers off or when Harriet the Hen no longer lays at least one egg per day, her days dwindle down. Bessie becomes hamburger; Harriet becomes the meat ingredient in chicken soup.

Bessie's and Harriet's lives would have been very different on traditional family farms, where cows, for example, generally have access to pasture and roam outside—within fences, of course. At Green Hills Harvest Farm in north central Missouri, laying hens peck at grasshoppers, beetles, and seeds around their mobile laying and roosting house. These are free-range chickens; their eggshells are brown, the yolks a vivid yellow. Over the millennia, farmers have learned that they cannot be overly sentimental about the animals they own. They know one day that fine fattening hog out in the pen will be gracing their or someone else's table. They know that today's free-range egg-layer will be tomorrow's chicken soup or baked hen. Nevertheless, farm animals are treated well on a traditional diversified farm. As Terry Spence, a farmer in northern Missouri who has a cow-calf operation, states, "Sure, I raise my calves for slaughter, but I don't torture them in the process."

In the concentrated animal feeding operations, animals are treated as nonsentient beings, as if incapable of feeling pain. Industrial agribusiness corporations have determined a measuring stick for proper population in a hog building, about eight square feet per hog. This measurement has been ascertained by observing what happens in the confinement building: If a hog doesn't get bitten or chewed on by other hogs, the density is not great enough; if a hog is fatally chewed or bitten or the bites decrease the value, the density is too great; if, however, a hog has bite marks on its back but not of a fatal nature, then the density is correct. In other words, the indicator is not whether the hog suffers bites from other hogs—apparently a certain amount is desirable—but to what degree the bites affect value. Lynn McKinley, who once raised hogs and now lives next door to buildings filled with corporate hogs, says that these animals scream: "They're in pain. It hurts me to listen to them." Rolf Christen, a farmer from northern Missouri, toured a massive finishing operation and was appalled by what he saw: "All the hogs in the building had cuts and sores on their backs; their tails were chewed. I couldn't believe my eyes. I knew it was bad in these buildings, but until this visit I really had no idea."

Most of us assume that dairies at least must provide pleasant places for cows. After all, a cow gives more milk when she's happy, right? Well, not quite. A cow gives more milk when given lots of water and appetite enhancers and not stressed too much. In today's allegedly "modern" dairies, where cows never touch green, growing grass but are contained in feedlots with easy access to abundant hay, grains, and water, cows live a short and unhappy life—judged by the standards of smaller and sustainable dairy farms in, for example, the upper Midwest. But they aren't tortured. Torture is not conducive to milk production.

That changes when a cow is no longer productive. For a relatively healthy cow, the end is no more (nor no less) brutal than for a steer. A short ride to the slaughterhouse, a stun gun to the brain, and death comes relatively quickly. Since computers keep track of milk production and cows are literally milked for all they are worth, cows are pretty much done in production-wise by the end of their third year and are culled from the herd. In Idaho, a large dairy and beef feedlot state, 65 percent of the cows slaughtered are dairy culls; only 35 percent are beef steers. But if the cow is not healthy, a different fate awaits. Slaughterhouses are mostly forbidden, some by their own policies, to take animals that are "3D"—dead, downed, or diseased. Since a downer cow, such as the one that contracted BSE in Washington State, is of substantially decreased value to the dairy owner, that animal is usually dragged off and buried, if it is too difficult to haul her to a slaughterhouse. If lucky, the cow will die prior to burial. One Idaho dairy was recently cited by that state's department of agriculture for burying at least one cow alive; scuff marks in the burial pit revealed that the cow had moved her legs after being covered with dirt. The dairy was fined $5,000.

In an attempt to bring the state's animal cruelty law up-to-date (the county prosecuting attorney would not at first even bring charges against the dairy owner), a committee of the Idaho General Assembly took up the matter. Large dairy farm owners testified that it was sometimes necessary to drag live cows behind tractors and that live burial was not uncommon. What became clear: A downed cow was of little value and could be treated accordingly. It was further revealed that farm animals are exempt from cruelty laws governing inhumane treatment. They can be treated or not treated any way at all— and while this may be immoral, unethical, and despicable, it is not illegal.

While broiler chickens' lives are brutish and short, as we shall see, laying hens endure more than any other farm animal. Most Americans with even passing concern have seen the photos of laying hens confined to tiny cages, heads sticking out, their feet entwined (sometimes permanently) in the steel mesh of the cage. A few years ago, a defunct egg-laying operation was visited by a photographer/reporter employed by a major newspaper. This facility, owned by a contract grower for one of the major egg companies, had been abandoned due to financial problems. The grower simply left, leaving 10,000 laying hens to die of starvation and dehydration. Neighbors had complained of an overpowering stench, and word had reached the newspaper a couple of years later. The newspaper asked the reporter to check this out during the course of his investigation into abuse of migrant workers by poultry slaughterhouses. Arriving at the site, the reporter pushed through tall weeds and squeezed through a broken door. He was greeted by the nightmarish sight of thousands of skeletal heads poking through rusted cages. There were thousands more feather-covered skeletons in the cages. Appalled by this vision of poultry hell, he dutifully took photos. When he submitted these along with his story, his editor told him that the photos could never be published in that newspaper. They were just too horrible and too graphic. The reporter argued his case. The photos revealed the reality of egg-laying operations, but they were not published and never have been. This reporter, a hardened investigative journalist, said recently that even after ten years he was still haunted by the image of those thousands of skulls sticking out through the cages.

And then there is what is, to me, the ultimate horror: veal. There is little to say that has not been said, but as I will show in the chapter on milk, it bears repeating. I intend this book to promote the purchase of meat, milk, and eggs that are raised in a nonindustrial setting and therefore to advocate humane and sustainable farming. There is simply no way to produce veal that does not involve cruelty.

## An Alien View

Not only does the agribusiness system treat animals as merely units of production, but the same attitude also extends to workers. I met a man, whom I will call Juan, who was recruited by a major meatpacking company. He crossed the border at

Juarez/El Paso without any documents such as a temporary visa, work permit, or green card. Juan climbed aboard a bus just across the bridge. The bus driver, who is also the recruiter, is paid up to $100 for each worker he delivers. On this particular day, the bus was filled—and the driver would collect $6,000 upon unloading the bus at the packing plant. While some illegal aliens pay large sums of money to "coyotes" who help them cross into the United States, American agribusinesses pay these bus drivers to do the work. In essence, they are just another form of "coyote."

Juan is a short, stocky, and very muscular fellow. Most of his bus-mates were of his age, midtwenties, and hungry for work. They were capable and able. Juan didn't expect to stay in the States for very long. The recruiter told Juan that he could make ten dollars per hour after a one-month trial period during which he would make seven dollars per hour. This was more than Juan could make in an entire day back home even at one of the maquiladoras (Mexican factories owned by foreign companies) in the border towns. If he took a job in one of these factories, he would be forced to live in a *colonia,* a collection of hovels lacking running water, electricity, or sanitary or cooking facilities. The recruiter for the packing plant had promised not only a high-paying job but also a modern apartment. Juan could live well and still send most of his salary home. He planned to return to his wife and small children after a year or so.

The reality Juan found was quite different from what he had been promised. He ended up sharing a cramped mobile home with five other migrant workers. There was indeed running water but no hot water. Electricity was available, but the workers had to make arrangements to put down a deposit and sign up for electric service. Due to, it said, the unstable and transient nature of their workforce, the electric utility company was unwilling to provide them with service. The workers who had arrived at the mobile home before Juan got there had grabbed the two small bedrooms. Juan slept on the sofa or on the floor with three others who had been on the bus with him. Nonetheless, his first and only check had $100 deducted from it for "lodging." "They charged me fifty dollars a week to sleep on the floor."

The work at the slaughterhouse was cold and hard. Juan's job all day, every day, was to trim fat from large cuts of meat. The line ran fast. He had to work quickly with a large knife. The line kept moving; it never stopped or slowed down. Juan could not take a break even to sharpen his knife or use the bathroom. He pissed down his pants at his workstation. By the end of his shift his knife blade became dull. Juan learned during his second week that a dull knife is dangerous indeed: While he was attempting to hold a slab of greasy meat and trim off the fat, his knife slipped and severed two of his fingers. They fell onto the worktable, became contaminated, and were not reattachable.

Then Juan learned something else: He had not worked at the packing plant long enough to acquire medical or health benefits, and he had no sick time coming to him. Not only was his pay terminated, but also he had to either pay for his medical costs, involving cauterization and suturing of the wounds where his two fingers once were, or rely on the free-services medical clinic located miles away, which accepted indigent patients.

When I first met Juan and he related to me his story, he was buying a bus ticket back to El Paso. Every dime he had earned during his short tenure at the plant went to purchasing transportation back home. His left hand was encased in bandages. He was very bitter. "My family was hungry; we were very poor. So, I came north. Big promises. Now, I am going back to my home with no money and with my fingers gone. What can I do now? I can't work here and with my hand like it is I can't find work in Mexico." There were two other men with Juan. Their tales were similar. They had been terminated, one because of recurring pains in his wrists and fingers and the other because he couldn't keep up with the line. They were going back home, broke and broken.

What happened to Juan and his companions is not uncommon. In fact, it is relatively standard. The large slaughterhouses/packing plants, though owned by some of the richest corporations in the world, have turnover rates of over 100 percent per year, due to hard work and low pay. It is common for landlords to make arrangements with the slaughterhouses for rent to come out of the check. The justification is that "these people are not dependable." The number of slaughterhouse workers with Hispanic surnames is over 65 percent. The Immigration and Naturalization Service (INS) recently accused Tyson of deliberately recruiting undocumented migrant workers for the company's packing plants. A jury in Chattanooga acquitted Tyson of all charges, citing that the evidence did not prove that company executives encouraged plant managers to do this. The slaughterhouse companies typically don't provide insurance benefits until an employee has been on the job for six months. Whether documented or undocumented, the workers file no claims for worker's compensation, file no complaints with OSHA (the Occupational Safety and Health Administration), and do not even join a union. Part of this is due to language barriers. But the larger part is due to intimidation. The United Food and Commercial Service Workers Union has for years been trying to organize employees at Smithfield Foods' Virginia and North Carolina slaughterhouses and has met with much resistance, including harassment and threats to employees, from the Smithfield management: "If you people know what's good for you, you won't be voting to join any union."

By relying on an alien workforce, unable to understand the language and with no experience and little training, the meatpacking companies have created work environments in which dangerous and unsanitary conditions are the norm. Juan and his fellow laborers are the human wreckage of a failed system.

## What Quality of Life?

"It used to be," proclaimed Jack Parrish, "that you would drive down the back roads here, and when you passed someone or saw someone sitting on their porch, you would wave and they'd wave back. No more. People aren't friendly anymore. No one knows whose side you're on."

Jack was born, raised, grew up, and still lives in Putnam County, Missouri. He never had much and never expected much. He was and is, by his account, "a poor country boy." But he did have friends and he knew almost everybody for miles around. Then, in 1989, Premium Standard Farms, Inc., a large agribusiness corporation, started moving into his area, and things changed rapidly. Some longtime farmers couldn't take the stink and the polluted waters, closed up, sold their farms, and moved out. Others bought air conditioners and locked themselves in their houses.

Premium Standard "Farms" experienced some financial difficulties and was bailed out by ContiGroup, one of the wealthiest agribusiness corporations in the world. Members of the board of directors are influential citizens such as Henry Kissinger, who has served for years. Premium Standard (aka ContiGroup) planned to raise 2.5 million hogs per year in Putnam, Mercer, and Sullivan counties, just south of the Iowa border. In the process of constructing and filling up the buildings with hogs, the company promised, it would bring jobs to the relatively few unemployed in the area. It did for a while, except that farmers don't make very good factory workers, and they soon learned that this was not a farm but a factory. Moreover, each concentration facility actually employed very few workers—five or six at the most—because everything was automated. The industry magazines touted this automation, boasting that things had "progressed to the point where a hog only needs individual worker attention for about 12 minutes in the entire finishing process."

Then Premium Standard Farms, Inc., spawned Premium Standard Foods, Inc., a slaughterhouse and packing plant in Milan, Missouri, a town of about five hundred. This slaughterhouse was set up to "disassemble"—the industry term for slaughtering and processing—7,000 hogs per day. To do the demanding, demeaning, cold, and cruel work of converting live animals into cellophane-wrapped products the company initially hired the local farmers they had put out of the hog-raising business. Again, farmers don't make very good factory workers. Today the company's employees are mostly Hispanic. Some have papers; some don't.

Problems soon started. Milan went from being a sleepy little town to one with gangs, drive-by shootings, spousal abuse, child abuse, and drug abuse. The Hispanic workers had no support system, and none was provided by the company. These were strangers in a strange land. The local churches tried to provide the very basics of life—food, clothing, and shelter—but the town was small and poor and the congregations were likewise. Rather than blaming the company for these problems, the result of bringing in an alien workforce and providing no support, some of the townspeople took out their frustrations on the workers. Still others, such as the local church leaders, called loudly and publicly for the company to take responsibility for the mess it had created.

This scenario gets repeated in every small town where large slaughterhouses have been established. The social support systems have been turned upside down, by being inundated with people who don't speak English, don't know local customs, and have no familiarity with the culture. Drug and alcohol abuse becomes widespread. Slaughterhouses, as we will see, desensitize and to an extent even dehumanize the workers. Employees spend an entire eight-hour shift killing and disassembling animals. What they experience carries over into other aspects of their lives. The community values are rent in twain. Neighbor turns against neighbor, friend against friend. You're either "pro" or "anti" CAFO; there's no in-between. Generally speaking, those whose business benefits from Premium Standard's presence are real estate brokers, convenience store owners, and equipment dealers. Longtime farmers are hostile and embittered. Since the companies involved are huge, with millions, even billions, in assets, it is unlikely that they will be brought down or run out by a few unhappy rural residents.

However, Jack Parrish and his neighbors won't quit. They show up at town meetings and present statements to state commissions and public officials. They file complaints and have become trained in air and water monitoring. They have banded together and filed lawsuits and administrative appeals. Their cry is, "We will not go away and we will not shut up." Rolf Christen, an acquaintance of Jack and a pillar in his community and in his church in Milan, puts it more succinctly: "No one, no one, *no one,* should have the right to stink me out of my house!" Rolf lives downwind from 80,000 hogs owned by Premium Standard. A native of Switzerland, Rolf has also endured xenophobic taunts and threats from some of his neighbors, most of whom make their living from Premium Standard.

Premium Standard has had difficulties reaching its goal of raising 2.5 million hogs per year. Production problems have led to layoffs. The Milan plant has never reached its maximum capacity of 7,000 hogs per day. Longtime farmers believe that a lack of diversity in breeds is one source of the problem. When all sows have the same genetic makeup, disease spreads quickly throughout the entire herd.

Once upon a time, every small town had a slaughterhouse. No one can claim that these operations didn't pose sanitation problems. By its very nature, killing and cutting up farm animals is a brutish enterprise and one that poses all sorts of sanitary challenges. As I will later show in greater and grislier detail, the stomachs and intestines of the animals must be removed, and these are laden with bacteria. Should the meat become contaminated via improper handling or exposure, those eating the meat will likewise be exposed. Animals' guts contain various pathogens. Normally these don't cause any problems, as long as they are not ingested by other animals, such as humans. Although imperfect, those small slaughterhouses sometimes created small outbreaks of disease—small because exposure to the contaminated meat was quite limited.

No longer. When ground beef is made up of the components of thousands of cows, the contamination, from bacteria contained in excrement and entrails, becomes rampant. For example, the slaughterhouse and packing plant in Greeley, Colorado, owned at the time by ConAgra, had to recall 18.6 million pounds of meats contaminated with *E. coli* (technically *E. coli* H7:1057) pathogens. The company was allegedly unaware of any problems with the meat until consumers became sickened. Instead of alerting consumers to potential harm, the USDA chose to conduct two more days of tests, during which time most of the contaminated meat was consumed. Victims, especially young children, suffered from severe gastroenteritis (including vomiting blood) and endured permanent injuries to vital organs, such as the liver and kidneys. A few died.

However, even in this highly publicized recall, only a small percentage of the ground beef was actually returned to the slaughterhouse. The *Denver Post* reported that a mere 12,000 pounds had been returned, though ConAgra had asked retailers and consumers to destroy suspect meat. The meat that was returned to the ConAgra plant was heated to destroy the bacteria and then resold. Much of the meat was placed in value-added products and recycled into supermarket cases in the form of spaghetti sauce, canned chili, and ravioli, among other items. Still, as one consumer put it, "It may be free of bacteria, but I don't want to eat poop."

Slaughterhouses no longer kill, cut up, and package meats for local families. Rather, these operations are massive facilities owned by the companies, such as Seaboard, Tyson, and IBP, which own the animals that are grown on contract. The numbers of animals killed and processed is truly astounding. The Tyson plant in Noel, Missouri, alone processes 300,000 chickens per day; a similar facility a few miles away and owned by Simmons Foods also processes 300,000 chickens per day. The Premium Standard Foods plant in the same state was designed to kill 7,000 hogs per day. Seaboard has been looking for a site for a plant that will kill 16,500 hogs per day; the current target is a tract of land just south of Dumas, Texas. The IBP slaughterhouse in Garden City, Kansas, disassembles 6,400 steers per day. The plant in Greeley, Colorado, formerly owned by ConAgra also kills and processes 6,400 steers per day. Each of these facilities keeps the production lines moving at a rate of 400 carcasses per hour and runs two eight-hour shifts per day—the so-called graveyard third shift is reserved for sanitation and maintenance.

With these numbers of animals being killed, skinned (or plucked), gutted, and cut into edible chunks, it is not at all surprising that sanitation crews simply cannot keep up. Workers at these plants complain about the speed of the line, and meat inspectors, always in short supply, can do little more than take occasional samples. Even when contaminated meats are pulled off the line, there are, as we will see, documented instances where these are put back on the line during the next shift.

The meat companies have, so far, managed to pass off responsibility to consumers for causing food-borne illnesses. Most restaurants will not cook steaks rare, advising patrons that doing so is unsafe. Even in the infamous Jack in the Box case, in which several people died and hundreds became sick, the meat industry blamed the fast-food chain, located in the Pacific Northwest, for improperly preparing its hamburgers. Rather than clean up its act and send uncontaminated meats into the marketplace, the packing companies advise consumers to prepare the meats in such a way as to destroy the pathogens.

## Some Antibiotics with Your Meal?

As I've suggested, farm animals destined to end up as food are fed copious quantities of antibiotics. Consequently, the very drugs that medical professionals rely upon to combat food-borne illnesses are no longer effective. The Union of Concerned Scientists reports that over 70 percent of antibiotics manufactured in this country are fed to farm animals. These antibiotics—the same ones that have proven so valuable in treating humans—are given "subtherapeutically" as appetite enhancers, not for disease.

It is hoped—there is no actual scientific proof—that antibiotics will somehow ward off the inevitable results of deplorable living conditions and stress and promote efficient growth. *Efficient* means that the animal will gain much weight on the smallest amount of feed. The problem is that a small daily dose of these antibiotics creates resistant pathogens in the guts of the animals. These pathogens—*E. coli*, salmonella, camphylobacter, and others—result in human illnesses. So two realities are at work: Meats get contaminated in vast quantities, and the antibiotics prescribed by doctors prove ineffective against the contaminants that cause the diseases that humans contract from eating contaminated meat. Sort of a Catch-22 situation.

There are certainly other abuses of antibiotics, including overprescription by doctors and the failure of individuals to take the prescribed dosages. But we should remember that use of antibiotics in nondiseased livestock—chickens, pigs, and cows—is eight times greater than among humans. Human antibiotic usage totals 3 million pounds per year; farmed animal usage is 25 million pounds per year. These tons of medicine are given to healthy animals—or at least as healthy as it is possible for an animal to be in the agribusiness system. It is the concentration of animals and consequent stress on them that prompts the use of antibiotics to enhance appetite and to promote more efficient conversion of feeds to weight gain. Farmers who raise animals in nonconfined ways tend not to use antibiotics. The Buckmeier family, owners of the aforementioned Green Hills Harvest Farm organic dairy in Linn County, Missouri, maintain that their pastured dairy cows have never been given antibiotics. Or as Barb Buckmeier states, "Our cows just don't get sick . . . and they produce plenty of milk."

McDonald's—the world's fast-food leader—issued a proclamation that it would not purchase chickens whose feeds contain a medically important antibiotic for "growth enhancement." Unfortunately, nice as it sounds, this will likely change little in the broiler industry. Read carefully, the wording in the Mc-

Donald's pronouncement says nothing about antibiotics used for disease prevention or other uses, only those used for growth enhancement. When 22,000 chickens are confined in a single building, there will always be at least one sick bird, thereby justifying the use of antibiotics to prevent the spread of disease and justifying the addition of antibiotics to feeds. Antibiotics, however, are effective only for combating actual diseases. They are not vaccines, which are preventive.

It is, to the distress of the agribusiness industry, the very methods of production used by corporate operations that lead to meats contaminated with the pathogens resistant to the specific antibiotics used to treat the diseases that humans contract from eating these meats. It is simply impossible to raise animals in concentrated operations and to slaughter these animals by the thousands or even the millions without severe health consequences among humans. By treating animals as units of production, the industrial methods, ultimately and inevitably, produce meats that are unfit to eat.

Ultimately, that is the lesson of the BSE outbreak. And it is the story behind the meat you eat.

# BIG PIG

"WE ONCE RAISED HOGS," SAYS LYNN MCKINLEY OF her and her husband, Jerry, "but we had to quit; there just wasn't any place to market them locally. We had to haul them up to Ottumwa in Iowa. That's about eighty miles away, and it took a lot of money to get them there.

"Then the price of hogs went way down," she adds, "to eight cents a pound. That's eight dollars per hundredweight. When you figure that a market-weight hog is about two hundred and fifty pounds, we were getting somewhere around twenty dollars for a full-grown pig. We had at least twice that much in the hog. We couldn't make any money. We couldn't eat all of our hogs, so we just hauled them all, including a couple of sows, up to Ottumwa, and we didn't get any more."

Lynn and Jerry have lived on the farm ever since they can remember. It has been in Jerry's family for several generations.

Jerry is not accustomed to speaking to anyone other than Lynn, and he doesn't say much. But whenever the subject of the industrial-hog operation next to their farm comes up, he hitches up his overalls, pulls his straw hat down over his forehead to cover up the red-hot anger, and it comes out: "They've just ruined this area. Everything around here just stinks. We never had air-conditioning before. When it got hot, we'd open the windows and turn on a fan. But now if you open the windows and the air is coming from that [he points to the silvery buildings across his pasture], you wake up gagging and choking. So, we got a window unit and we keep it turned on.

"I didn't know how bad it was, I guess you kind of get used to it, until one Sunday we were going into town to church and we stopped to give a ride to this widow lady that lives down the road a ways. She started to get in our car, and she stopped. 'What's that smell?' she said, and she told us our car smelled like hog crap. We can't get it out. The smell is in the upholstery. I guess we smell bad, too."

Lynn, red hair tucked in under a scarf, and short and petite in contrast to Jerry's stocky build, is not nearly as shy and reticent as Jerry. Standing in the building on their farm where their sows and boars were once housed, she sniffs the air and listens for a moment to the sounds of hogs in their concentration building across the field. "Listen to that! That's the sound of hogs in pain. They bite one another something awful. They all end up with big gashes and scars on their backs. Of course, the company doesn't mind this because it doesn't lower the price of meat at all. But, it hurts me to have to listen to that squealing all day. That is not the sound of a hungry hog—I know that sound. That's the sound of a hurting hog, and it hurts me.

"The company just doesn't care. They don't care if their stink is forcing us to shut up our house. They don't care if they're polluting the creeks and our wells. They don't care if their hogs are getting bitten. All they care about is how much money they make.

"Well, we raised hogs for money, too. We have needs for things that we can't grow or make. But we can't raise hogs any-more and make anything. They've seen to that. They won't take our hogs, not unless we'd sign a contract with them and do things their way. We'll never do that. I've seen their way, and it is not our way. Their way of making money smells al-most as bad as their hog operations."

And smell bad they do. The lawyer retained by Premium Standard Farms, Inc., the biggest hog company in Missouri, attends the regular meetings of the state's Clean Water Com-mission and Air Conservation Commission. He shows up in his pin-striped suit, and, though he doesn't know it, he reeks. Everyone knows when he enters the room because the stench of hog manure precedes him. He thinks people are joking when they tell him this and assumes that they are making pointed remarks about his clients.

In the mideighties, Rolf and Ilsa Christen, both originally Swiss, purchased a large farm north of Green City, Missouri, and moved into the comfortable farmhouse. They are both well educated. Rolf, a trained and certified engineer, says, "We sought out a place where we could farm and live in peace. We thought we had found it—rolling green hills, fertile soil, good neighbors. And we lived in peace for a long time. Then, in 1994, Premium Standard Farms moved in and set up a huge eighty-thousand-hog operation just west of my farm. Every reason that we had come here was ruined.

"I have fought them and failed all the way. I was in opposition to their construction. I tried to get the state and the federal government to put some restrictions on the operations to protect our air and water. We, along with about thirty other families, sued them. For a while, the EPA and the Justice Department were on our side. Then Bush came in and there was a settlement agreement that did nothing. They sold us out.

"I never heard one word about my accent or where I had come from until we got into this battle. Now, my citizenship and my patriotism are called into question. All of a sudden my wife and I are 'foreigners.' Well, I've been here for more than twice as long as Premium Standard Farms. So, who is the 'foreigner'? This big company has deprived me of clean air, clean water, peace, and solitude. My life has been turned upside down."

Rolf and Ilsa have talked of selling their farm and moving on but have rejected this notion: "We're sticking it out. They can't keep doing what they have been doing. They can't sustain it. You hear a lot about 'sustainable farming.' Well, what they're doing is the opposite of that. So, we'll wait and we'll keep trying to get the state and federal agencies to do something, and we'll probably sue the company again. Sooner or later, they'll give us our lives back."


The Texas Panhandle is flat. County and township roads don't curve; they run straight and true. In fact, it is possible to drive all the way across the Panhandle from New Mexico to Oklahoma without losing the "east" indicator on the dashboard compass. While the land is relatively featureless, there are a few canyons created by what passes for "rivers," and it has long been occupied by ranchers engaged in raising cattle and grains who are fiercely protective of this flatland. Their ownership is not measured in acres but in "sections," a square mile or 640 acres. In this part of the world, if you don't own at least two sections you don't count for much.

There's something new going on in the Texas Panhandle, an area that has changed little in the past century. Seaboard, Inc., has its eyes and money on locating a 16,500-hog-per-day slaughterhouse just south of Dumas. (Texans call it DumbAss, but non-Texans should refrain.) To slaughter this many hogs, this facility will require at least 4 million gallons of water every day. Slaughterhouses need a lot of water—about 250 gallons per animal—to wash the carcasses and to keep the equipment sanitized. Dumas has made commitments to supply water for the slaughterhouse, but it is far from certain whether water can be pumped in this quantity from the Ogallala Aquifer; it is certain, however, that this use will compete with area irrigation farmers.

If the slaughterhouse consumes 4 million gallons of water per day, it will also discharge that amount. While the company will have a wastewater treatment plant, these are notoriously vulnerable to upsets, as they are termed, occasions when the bacteriological and mechanical actions that clean the wastewater stop working because of malfunction or "operator error." When this happens, thousands, perhaps millions, of gallons of raw sewage, blood, grease, and other unsavory and harmful contaminants get released. The creek into which the slaughterhouse wastes will flow runs into Lake Meredith, the drinking-water supply lake for the city of Amarillo; the lake is also a major recreation area for water-skiers, swimmers, boaters, and anglers.

Water quantity and quality are critical issues for Panhandle area farmers and ranchers. But they are preoccupied with a more immediate problem. Seaboard is methodically purchasing hundreds of tracts of lands throughout the region between the Oklahoma state line and the Canadian River. Their plan is to construct concentrated animal feeding operations on each of these 40-to-160-acre tracts. These operations will "feed the mill," that is, provide the 16,500 hogs per day to the slaughterhouse near Dumas.

A brief word about the lands Seaboard is acquiring. Two modes of agriculture dominate the Texas Panhandle: irrigated farming and beef feedlots. Both require a great deal of water. However, the water required to furnish the feedlots' steers is not at stake. Irrigated farming is another issue. The center-pivot irrigation systems—those gigantic circles you see from a plane on a clear day—in the Panhandle are a half mile long, and the circle they cover is one mile in diameter. As I've noted, the tracts are divided into 640-acre square grids (one mile by one mile). The result is a circle in a square, and the irrigated circle does not extend into the corners of the square. Therefore, in each irrigated square mile there are four forty unirrigated corner acres. That's one forty-acre tract in each of the four corners, since the center of the center pivot is located exactly in the middle of each section. These unirrigated acres are of no value to the irrigation farmer—and they can be bought real cheap. Each of these forty-acre tracts does possess something quite valuable: water rights. Wells can be drilled. Texas water laws do establish some limits (although such laws are notoriously arcane, complicated, confusing, and even contradictory) on drilling into the Ogallala Aquifer, but no metering of pumps is required.

An individual hog requires about thirty-five gallons per day for drinking and to flush its wastes. A facility containing 20,000 hogs would therefore require about seven hundred thousand gallons per day. Removing this amount from the Ogallala Aquifer would create what hydrologists call a cone of depression, an inverted pyramid from which groundwater is temporarily depleted. The wells that furnish water for the irrigation pumps would most likely be sucking sand. That has local farmers and ranchers deeply concerned. Their livelihood is being threatened to ensure a profit for Seaboard.

Running a few numbers on the calculator quickly reveals that once the Seaboard slaughterhouse is up and running at full tilt, it will be able to handle 6 million hogs per year. These hogs will be raised throughout the Panhandle on those 40-to-160-acre tracts. The operations will inevitably be upwind of longtime farmers and ranchers. Ranchers Clarence and Marilyn Yanke recently abandoned their plans to restore and move into a large abandoned house on one of their ranches when they learned that Seaboard had obtained a permit to establish a large hog operation just to the west of them, upwind. Local farmers and ranchers have formed an organization called the Panhandle Alliance, which has opposed each of the permits Seaboard has sought for its operations, but the Texas Commission on Environmental Quality (TCEQ, formerly TNRCC, tagged "train wreck" by some), the state agency that awards such permits, has turned a deaf ear to assertions of detrimental impact on air, water, and quality of life. One petition circulated by "ACCORD" in opposition to a non-Seaboard 10,000-sow/farrowing operation near Pampa, about sixty miles east of Dumas, was signed by 1,500 local residents yet completely ignored by the TCEQ.

Similar stories are told by rural residents from coast to coast. From Smithfield's hog operations in the watershed of North Carolina's Neuse River to a gigantic hog facility near San Diego in Ramona, California, money talks and local residents' concerns get ignored. It is unusual to the point of being an anomaly for a permit to be denied, no matter how damaging the operation will prove to local waterways, how fouled the air becomes, or how many area residents object to it. What Big Pig wants, Big Pig gets.

### Aiders and Abettors

How did things get this way? Part of the blame must go to governmental agencies, including federal- and state-funded public universities, which have aided and abetted Big Pig.

I've mentioned several times the role agriculture departments at state universities have played in supporting the "Get Big or Get Out" philosophy. Introduced by Justin Smith Morrill of Vermont, the Land-Grant College Act of 1862 provided funding for institutions of higher learning. Each state in the union was to receive 30,000 acres of federal land for each congressional representative from that state; the land was to be sold and the proceeds used to provide an endowment for "at least one college where the leading object shall be, without excluding other scientific and classical studies and including military tactics, to teach such branches of learning as are related to agriculture and the mechanic arts." These public institutions were given three missions by Congress:

1. To provide a practical, affordable college-level education in agriculture and other subjects being missed by private universities.

2. To conduct research on topics related to agriculture.

3. To disseminate research findings to the public in a form that nonscientists could understand and put to use.

These are very broad charges, but one mandate is clear: The land-grant universities were to provide a public benefit.

Colleges of agriculture at these land-grant universities established departments to assist in developing new agriculture techniques. By the end of World War II, nearly all of these departments became focused on agribusiness industries and began to view, and still view, farming as a business. Most managed to conceal this bias; others didn't bother. At institutions as diverse as North Carolina State, the University of Florida, Texas Agriculture and Mining University, and the University of Missouri the colleges formed overtly commercial agriculture departments. And faculties within these departments make no pretense about their goals. They are involved in research and development for industrial agribusiness. Faculty at the University of Missouri, for example, claim to have developed the system of commercial hog production and lagoon-and-spray field manure handling (a claim disputed by many others, including Wendell Murphy, the North Carolina state senator, who became known as "Boss Hog"). Currently, however, these dedicated scientists are helping the NRCS devise standards for determining how much hog crap can be applied to farmlands and still not exceed the "agronomic rate," which they view as the point at which manure is applied so thickly that it runs off. These scientists, or biostitutes, as I've said they're sometimes called, get grants from agribusiness corporations and the USDA for such services, of course. Since their services are for hire, these scientists act as shills for industrial hog operations at local, state, and federal hearings. They have submitted expert testimony that hog shit doesn't stink and wastes don't pollute water and touted the economic efficiency of such commercial operations. Many of these departments received grants from the very entities whose operations they have touted.

Land-grant colleges and universities don't assist small or diversified farms; there's no money in it. When the students in one large seminar class on animal science at an agricultural college were asked whether they had read works by Wendell Berry, Wes Jackson, or Gene Logsdon (all advocates of small, diversified farms), they answered with blank stares. They had mastered the lexicon of agribusiness industry but had given no attention either to the needs of the land or to anyone engaged in sustainable farming. This comes as no surprise. Even a cursory glance at the course offerings and descriptions at any college of agriculture will reveal that they are almost totally focused on agribusiness and the agribusiness industry. Large agribusiness companies recruit eager agriculture graduates. Most "aggies" end up working for Monsanto, Tyson, or Novartis; very few end up tilling the soil.

As at the ag schools, the mission of the USDA is to promote production while paying at least token attention to conserving natural resources. However, neither the USDA nor its subsidiary the NRCS is in the business of regulation. The NRCS is the technical assistance and grant-making arm of the USDA, providing on-the-ground help—and buckets of money—to favored agribusinesses but not at all interested in promoting, assisting, or financing small-farm operations or sustainable agriculture. The Environmental Working Group's database of farm subsidies (available at www.ewg.org) reveals that the largest checks go to those with the most acreage and the most production. The subsidies doled out by the USDA likewise benefit primarily those who are already rolling in high clover. Both the USDA and the NRCS tend to give their grants and subsidies to those least in need yet who produce the most. This creates a vicious cycle of overproduction. There have been valiant attempts by brave—or foolish—U.S. representatives and senators to base subsidies on need or conservation, but to date those efforts have enjoyed about as much success as Don Quixote had in defeating the windmills.

So it is with hogs. To cite but one example, the Farm Bill, a federal act that gets renewed every five years, contains a program titled Environmental Quality Improvement Program, which goes by its acronym of EQIP or, simply, "Equip." This program was established to provide grants to smaller, independent farmers for conservation projects, like buffer strips along streams. In the 1995 Farm Bill, environmental, conservation, and sustainable agriculture groups were successful in keeping any of the EQIP grants from flowing to "large" animal feeding operations. After much pressure, the secretary of agriculture decreed that *large* was to be defined as 1,000 or more animal "units," the size for which the Clean Water Act requires wastewater discharge, National Pollution Discharge Elimination System, permits. The decree was a victory for sustainable agriculture groups, since it meant that EQIP grants, which would pay out $60 million per year by 2001, could not be given to large agribusiness corporations. Almost all of the agribusinesses' operations have considerably more than 1,000 animal units.

Alas, in the 2002 Farm Bill that passed through the Congress and was signed into law by President Bush there is no such prohibition against "large" operations receiving EQIP funds. To the contrary, the administration argued that in order to comply with new regulations by the EPA, large livestock operations needed access to these funds. Having failed to secure a prohibition, sustainable ag groups then lobbied for a $50,000-per-operation limit. Congress debated this for quite some time and finally imposed a total limit—of $450,000 per owner. Finally, sustainable ag lobbyists tried to prevent EQIP grants from going to "new or expanded CAFOs." This effort also failed. As if to rub salt in the wounds of sustainable agriculture, NRCS decided that 60 percent of EQIP funds should be directed to "animal operations." Large grants are now going to install new or expanded lagoon systems or even to build new confinement facilities.

The EPA is a regulatory body, responsible, as we've seen, for administering the Clean Air Act, the Clean Water Act, the Safe Drinking Water Act, the Resource Conservation and Recovery Act (Hazardous Waste), and all the other human health and natural resource protective laws. The EPA is the nation's watchdog, ensuring that industries are polluting within limits established by laws and implementing regulations. But agriculture has been exempt from most of these laws, which were enacted in simpler times, when traditional farmers did minimal damage to human health or natural resources and when it was deemed in the national interest to promote agricultural practices. To cite but a couple of examples, there is an exemption for "agricultural storm water," so that any runoff from farm fields is exempt from water pollution laws, and there is an exemption from "fugitive dust" emission, meaning that agricultural dust is not deemed to be an air contaminant as defined by the Clean Air Act. There are similar exemptions to other provisions of environmental laws. The use of pesticides and herbicides is administered by the USDA or the agriculture departments of the states, and these agencies are more inclined to overlook infractions than to enforce procedures.

It is no accident, then, that Big Pig acts as any industry but gets itself legally categorized as "agriculture." Even a hog operation with 100,000 animals is legally considered a "farm."

In addition to the legal loopholes protecting Big Pig, the industry has powerful political connections, making it difficult for the EPA to regulate it. Indeed, the EPA has yielded to pressure by representatives of the National Pork Producers. It is no longer agency policy to take any enforcement actions against hog CAFOs. State legislators have similarly shown little or no interest in bringing Big Pig under control. Indeed, they have tried to take away the small amount of authority that the counties still retain to place protective restrictions on hog operations. In several states, most recently Pennsylvania and Texas, legislators under the sway of the Farm Bureau and the state affiliates of the Pork Producers Council have introduced bills to require that counties' ordinances can be "no stricter than state law"—never mind that these state laws either have no teeth or are nonexistent.

A few brave state legislators have introduced legislation to place controls upon hog CAFOs and have seen their bills weakened to the point where the legislation actually offers incentives to locate operations in that state. Only in a few states, such as Oklahoma and Kansas, where problems simply could not be ignored, have actions been taken to prevent or minimize damage to human health and natural resources.

## An Integrated System

The "pork powerhouses," listed in appendix A, have bought into the system first developed by John Tyson, founder of Tyson Foods. These companies boast about "vertical integration," claiming that controlling the entire process, from feed mill to retail product, helps maintain quality and uniformity. There is some truth to this: The pork chops produced by this system are uniform in size, shape, and leanness. The meats are also bland to the point of being tasteless, in addition to being laced with pathogens resistant to antibiotics.

Each company controls every aspect of hog production. First of all, the companies own the feed mills and put in all the ingredients. Each company claims those ingredients are its secret to efficient hog production and therefore that the feeds are "proprietary." What is known is that these companies add various heavy metals and antibiotics as growth enhancers and for "subtherapeutic" purposes. Second, the company owns the breeding stock. Unfortunately for the poor sow, she never meets the boar. The boar is manually masturbated by women, who, hog companies assert, have the "right touch." The semen is collected and artificially introduced into the sow. No joy of sex in this process. Third, the company owns the sow and ultimately the piglets. Much has been written about the gestation crates in which the sow is imprisoned, and I will add more to it later. Fourth, the company owns the pigs throughout the process of "finishing" or attaining a weight of about 250 pounds for slaughter. The company dictates to its employees or contract growers the daily management activities in the CAFOs in which the hogs are grown to finished size. The company determines when the hogs are to be picked up or delivered for slaughter. The company owns the slaughterhouse and packing plant in which the hogs are disassembled and packaged for retail sale. And, in most instances, the company owns the refrigerated trucks that deliver the packaged meat products to the retail outlet.

This complete control ensures that every piece of meat—ham, pork chop, bacon—is virtually identical to every other piece. To attain maximum speed at the slaughterhouse and packing plant, hogs need to be roughly the same size and confirmation. That is why every animal is of the same breed, is fed the same food—and at the same rate—and ideally reaches the magic size at the same time.

These companies use three different business models:

1. *The company owns and operates it all.* This model was used almost exclusively by Premium Standard Farms and Smithfield during their initial growth phase.

2. *The company contracts with farmers to raise the hogs.* This model is preferred by Seaboard, Pig Improvement Company, and Swine Graphics (the actual names of agribusiness hog companies), as the major liabilities accrue to the grower, and the company reaps all the benefits.

3. *A combination of the preceding two models.* This third option is becoming quite common. Companies such as Premium Standard and Smithfield have adopted the contract system in order to expand and avoid the high price of land in the Midwest and Atlantic states. Conversely, the "contract companies" have been forced to grow their own animals due to a shortage of farmers willing to sign one-sided contracts in areas of the country that Seaboard has targeted (for example, the Texas Panhandle).

It matters little to consumers which model dominates the industry: The pork it produces will be uniform. And vertical integration assures one other thing, a fact documented by the Centers for Disease Control (CDC): It will also be potentially harmful to human health.

### "It Doesn't Smell like Money. It Just Stinks"

Hog manure has a particularly nasty odor. The feces of other animals may not exactly smell like roses, but no other excrement approaches hog poop in sheer offensiveness. A few hogs can create a stink. A few thousand hogs will overwhelm the neighborhood. As I've mentioned, there are some who claim to have solved the so-called odor problem with large hog operations. Even the most optimistic sales representatives won't claim to make the smell disappear, instead asserting that their solution will "cut the odor in half." So the reply is, "You can make eighty thousand hogs smell like forty thousand. Big deal." At this point, the sales rep wilts and disappears.

If the odor problem could be resolved, it is likely that opposition to Big Pig would be much reduced. The ranchers in the Texas Panhandle are accustomed to the smell of beef feedlots, and these to an uninitiated nose smell pretty bad. But the smell is not overwhelming or so offensive that dinners, clothes, car upholstery, and sleep are ruined. At the West Texas town of Hereford (its real name), beef feedlots quite literally surround the town and there are, by last count, three beef slaughterhouses with "holding pens." There are few complaints. (See appendix A for a listing of feedlots.)

Other towns are similarly situated: Greeley, Colorado, has a massive feedlot more or less in the center of town. It doesn't smell good, but, in the words of a longtime resident, "it can be tolerated." While there are other problems with this operation (as we will see in "Big Beef"), longtime citizens of Greeley have learned to live with the odor. Newcomers, who apparently moved in when the wind blew the smell the other way, have filed complaints—but the response has generally and rightly been: "The feedlot was there first."

Not so with hogs. Recently there has been a move to place large hog feeding operations in sparsely populated areas. Milford Valley, Utah, the Panhandle of Texas, the eastern plains of Colorado, North Dakota, and the prairie provinces of Canada have all been targeted by the hog agribusiness companies as good places to locate hog operations. Much to the consternation and frustration of the hog companies, there were longtime ranchers and farmers in every place where the CAFOs went in and they encountered opposition even in such sparsely populated areas as were chosen. In Milford Valley, a group of ranchers have filed a nuisance lawsuit against Smithfield, the only company remaining of the original four of Circle Four after Smithfield acquired the shares of the other three companies. In this rural and sparsely populated valley in central Utah, hidden from the view of the world in its fold between two mountain ranges, the stink of hundreds of thousands of hogs overwhelms the desert air. There is literally no place in North America where a hog operation can be located without offending the inhabitants—every place has residents and all those residents have noses.

Moreover, the hog companies chose to locate first in popu-

lated areas with lots of people who didn't appreciate the stink.
Even in Iowa, the longtime leader in hog production, organized opposition to the massive hog feeding operations arose.
These were not, as the hog companies like to claim, "move-
ins"—city dwellers who had moved to the country—but rather
old-time farmers and longtime rural residents who were certainly accustomed to the fresh country air with the occasional
aroma of manure but who objected long and loud to the overwhelming stink of thousands of hogs.

Other states in which the hog companies found a hostile re-
ception from residents were North Carolina (inadvertently
scaring the neighboring state of South Carolina into passing
prohibitive laws) and the midwestern states of Ohio, Indiana,
Kentucky, Illinois, Missouri, Kansas, and Oklahoma. Finding
that state legislators were of little help, several counties in
these states crafted their own protective ordinances. Some required setbacks from occupied residences; some flatly banned
CAFOs; others decreed these to be predictive nuisances. Finally, state legislatures in North Carolina and Oklahoma
passed moratoria banning new or expanded hog operations.

The hog companies also found themselves under siege in
midwestern and eastern seaboard states and spending considerable time defending themselves in court. They therefore
went shopping for places where there were complacent or eas-
ily purchased politicians and few rural residents. The only
problem was that, as noted, there is almost no place in North
America without people, or local county commissions unre-
sponsive to citizen requests and demands. Unfortunately for
Big Pig, its reputation preceded it.

The only place left seemed to be the Intermountain West,

where livestock producers have long been operating. These states, Utah, Idaho, Montana, Arizona, and New Mexico, have few or no laws on livestock production. The hog companies are gambling that their lobbyists and the lobbyists for other agribusiness organizations, the Farm Bureau, and the Cattlemen's Beef Association can stave off bans, moratoria, and restrictive regulations until they get settled in. Once in place, they'll have ten or twenty years to comply with any new laws or regulations, since existing facilities are normally "grandfathered in" and given a long period of time to come into compliance; new operations must do so immediately.

## A Pig's Life

What is it like inside Big Pig? The lives of the animals resemble those of chickens, dairy cows, or steer—that is, they are considered "units" rather than living creatures. A piglet never gets to snuggle up to its mother but recognizes the mother sow only by her teats. You see, the sow is encased in a metal cage, the idea being to prevent her from rolling onto her brood. There is nothing particularly new about this. Long ago, hog farmers devised contraptions to keep newborn piglets from being crushed or smothered by the sow. The difference is that in today's sow and farrowing operations the piglets are prevented from *any* motherly contact and are separated from the mother sow at an early age.

During pregnancy, the sow is encased in a gestation crate, intended to keep her completely immobile. This crate, by the way, was recently banned in the state of Florida by a ballot vote; Floridians deemed it cruel and inhumane. However, the vote has not put an end to farrowing crates, which are used as long as the piglets are with the sow. At one to four days of age—depending on the hog operation's schedule—the piglets get "processed": Their tails are docked, their ears are notched as a form of branding, they are castrated if male, their newborn, needle-sharp teeth are trimmed or filed, and they are given shots to stimulate growth. At three weeks of age, they leave the mother sow and are sent off to get fattened. The sow is immediately artificially inseminated and begins the next cycle of gestation.

When the pigs reach fifty-five pounds or so, they are transported to the next-to-final stop, the so-called finishing operation. Typically, the hogs are housed in buildings that hold anywhere between 1,100 and 2,500 animals; the average site has six to ten such buildings. These buildings have slatted floors through which the waste falls. A flush system carries the waste to a gigantic cesspit. These pits, euphemistically and hopefully called lagoons by the hog companies, are up to twenty-five feet deep and up to eighteen acres in size. Typically, each cesspit holds the wastes of the six to ten buildings at the site and is roughly the size of a football field. As the cesspits reach capacity, a fixed irrigation piping system delivers the liquefied manure and urine to the adjacent fields, where those center-pivot or "manure cannons" send the wastes into the fields.

The operation's goal is, always and ever, efficiency—so that the hogs reach market size of about 250 pounds in the least amount of time and with the least amount of feed. Unfortunately for both the hogs and the growers, the stress generated by such congestion and such massive feed intake results in a high mortality rate, apparently roughly 12 percent from weaning to finishing on an industry average, although rates as high as 15 percent are not uncommon. Smaller dead hogs don't pose any serious disposal problems; a 200-pound carcass is another matter. Various solutions have been provided by agricultural researchers, from incineration, to burial, to composting, but none have worked particularly well. This problem is compounded by ownership of the hog magically being transferred to the contract grower upon the death of the animal. The dead hog provides no benefits to the grower. It is merely a liability. Sociable and gregarious by nature, hogs do not fare well in congested conditions. Hence the need for the appetite and growth enhancers and antibiotics.

From squeal to meal, from semen to cellophane, the life of a pig is carefully controlled and managed by those whose only interest is profit. The animals are transformed into eating machines that can be converted into meat. At the end of a rather miserable existence—hogs are also quite intelligent, though of course intelligence has no value in this system—the day arrives when the hog reaches market weight and gets hauled off to the slaughterhouse and packing plant.

# BIG CHICKEN AND BIG EGG

## Big Chicken

"JOHN SMITH," A CONTRACT GROWER WHO WAS ALSO A state legislator, told me that he had once taken the time to determine what he earned from his "chicken man" wages. It was $2.25 per hour. His original contract was with Hudson, but when Tyson acquired that company they acquired its contracts as well. Smith couldn't run for reelection because he couldn't afford to hire farm laborers—who wants to work for $2.25 per hour?—and needed to tend to his flock. He regretted deeply that he had ever signed the contract and mortgaged his farm to construct the facilities. "Now, I'm stuck," said Smith. "What can be done with chicken houses except raise chickens? I have a loan payment each year of one hundred and twenty-five thousand dollars, and the only way that can be paid off is to keep raising chickens."

John Tyson of Springdale, Arkansas, as noted previously, started the move toward "vertical integration" in the poultry industry back in the late 1950s. Throughout the 1930s and 1940s he had been struggling to make a living, hauling the products of his and his hens' labors to the towns of northwest Arkansas. Then he learned that more money was to be made by delivering chickens to Kansas City and St. Louis and eventually to Chicago and other northern cities. John began hauling chickens from other local chicken farmers to these markets. In the early 1950s, his son Don joined the commercial egg and broiler business.

The terrain of northwest Arkansas, rugged hills, steep slopes, deep V-shaped valleys, didn't lend itself to row cropping. There was some timbering, but landowners didn't like clear cuts on their lands and were reluctant to allow Weyerhauser or the other large logging companies to come on their properties. But the unemployment rate was very high in Arkansas and particularly so in the northwest. There were, however, a large number of small landholdings. These were not really farms, since little could be grown on them. Those with holdings of unproductive lands but with no goods to sell were known as land-poor.

Most of the landowners were subsistence farmers, raising chickens, cows, and pigs for their own consumption and relying on vegetable gardens to provide fresh produce in the summer and canned goods in the winter. For cash, well, there wasn't much. Surplus meat, milk, and eggs were sold locally or in nearby towns. There often wasn't much surplus. This was the setting greeting veterans returning from foreign wars: a pleasant land with lots of hills, trees, wild animals, and clear flowing streams and no way to make a living.

But chicken houses, confining thousands of birds in a semi-climate-controlled building, could be constructed anywhere there was an acre or so of flat ground. After John Tyson had started to haul the chickens and eggs to market, an industry was born, and northwest Arkansas became the epicenter for the poultry industry.

Eventually, Tyson got incorporated, and Tyson Foods, Inc., began acquiring other poultry companies and buying out poultry producers. By the early 1960s, the company was in control of the entire process from feed mills, to hatcheries, to growing houses, to processing plants, to delivery, to retail outlets. By 1970, broiler sales had reached 72 million chickens and for the first time Tyson appeared on the Fortune 1000 list. It was no longer hauling live chickens to cities of the North; now it was supplying chicken parts to the entire country.

At some point in the process of getting big, Tyson Foods, Inc., discovered that it was cheaper to contract with local farmers and let them raise the broilers than to do it itself. The advantages to the company were immense. They could let the contract growers assume all the risks and the company would still reap the benefits. The terms of the contracts to which Tyson submits its growers are not negotiable. Either the grower accepts and signs the contract as is or there is no arrangement. To a local farmer, it sounds good at first: Tyson will provide the chicks, Tyson will provide the feeds, and Tyson will pick up the birds when they reach market size (it only takes six or seven weeks from chicks to broilers). The grower is guaranteed a price for each bird that reaches a pre-determined weight by the pickup date. What most growers don't realize until after the contract is inked is that they have just signed away their freedom. They become, as one of them phrased it, serfs on their own land.

The contract terms are standard throughout the industry. The representatives of Big Chicken speak in glowing terms of the benefits to the growers. Growers soon discover reality is considerably less lustrous. They have to construct the confinement buildings with feed conveyors, fans, screens, and canvas window coverings, as well as other appurtenances detailed in the contract. Each such setup costs about one hundred thousand dollars per building and the average grower needs ten buildings. Coming up with a million dollars in northwest Arkansas almost always involves a bank loan secured by the contract grower's lands. Initially, Tyson Foods, Inc., would cosign the loan. This was stopped after it wound up owning huge acreages and assuming a lot of debt.

Other terms in the contract dictate the day-to-day management of the operation. Disposal of waste products is the grower's responsibility. When chickens die before the pickup date, disposal of the carcasses is up to the grower. Disposal is no small task. Mortality rates can run as high as 20 percent of a flock, and in the event of a disease outbreak or natural disaster such as a tornado, heat wave, or snowstorm an entire operation's flock may be wiped out.

The bizarre situation confronting contract growers is that while they have made the decision to stay down on the farm and Tyson seemed to have offered a way to do that, they are no longer farmers. Rather, they are chicken caretakers. Every waking moment is devoted to taking care of the chickens. Moreover, the growers have literally bet the farm, normally for a period of fifteen to thirty years. Initially, the growers' contracts were for three years and taking out a fifteen-year loan based on a three-year contract did not seem like a very good idea. Now the contracts are flock-to-flock and if the grower does not perform, the contract may be canceled. Nonperformance, however, is not based on following the day-to-day management procedures stipulated by the contract; it is determined by how many chickens reach the desired weight by the pickup date, a date over which the grower has absolutely no control.

And that is the essential problem with this whole arrangement: The grower is powerless. If the chicks that are delivered to his operation are puny or sickly, if the feeds are subpar, if the appetite enhancers and antibiotics are not added to feeds in the correct amounts, or if a disease or disaster wipes out a considerable portion or the entire flock, the grower will not meet the performance standard. Yet these things are beyond the control of the grower. His fate is in someone else's hands. Moreover, as 200 growers for Tyson found out in 2002, the company can cancel the contract for no reason at all, or at least no reason that has anything to do with meeting performance standards. The contract stipulates that should the company's mission change due to financial exigencies, the company may simply notify the grower that the contract is canceled. And, as Smith, the state legislator and poultry grower, found out, there is nothing that can be done with chicken houses except . . . raise chickens. If the contract is canceled, there is no way to pay off the loan on the buildings and the grower can lose the farm.

In addition to all of these contractual difficulties, the grower is at the mercy of the company, which determines the number of chickens it wants delivered to the slaughterhouse and the average weight per bird. There have been allegations that the company cheats on numbers and weights and lawsuits have been filed, but it is unlikely that the litigants will receive any more flocks. Dissension is not tolerated. When two Tyson contract growers attended the Plains Truth conference, dedicated to fending off corporate intrusions into agriculture, in Oklahoma City a few years ago, they did so with paper bags over their heads and refused to identify themselves. They were afraid that if Tyson company managers learned of their attendance at this conference, they would lose their contracts, their livelihood, and their farms.

The USDA and NRCS have a considerable degree of complicity in this system. Indeed, some would claim that they have been in bed with the large agribusiness corporations. There are some valid reasons for this. It is always easier to deal with a few "professional" officers of large companies or agribusiness organizations than with un- or disorganized farmers' groups. If, for example, the National Pork Producers Council (NPPC) strikes a deal with the USDA/NRCS the agencies can be assured that all of the hog companies will stick to this agreement. Likewise, if the INS files a lawsuit against Tyson, the INS can be sure that all of Tyson's operations will adhere to a settlement agreement. But if the USDA/NRCS meets with representatives of the Midwest Sustainable Agriculture Working Group and arrives at an accord over some contentious issue, the MSAWG cannot assure the agency that all of its members will buy into this agreement. Indeed, since farmers have historically been such an independent lot, it is relatively safe to assume that no one organization can speak for individual farmers. The USDA/NRCS leadership would prefer to deal with those who can provide assurances to the agency that their members will fall into line. Consequently, the NPPC, the Farm Bureau, the Cattlemen's Beef Association, and the other agribusiness commodity groups and a few CEOs of large agribusiness corporations have frequent meetings with the various program or division heads in the EPA, USDA, and USDA/NRCS.

### A BROILER CHICKEN'S LIFE

On the banks of the Elk River in Noel, Missouri, is a massive Tyson Foods, Inc., poultry slaughterhouse and processing plant. This facility kills, packs, and ships 300,000 chickens per week. This means that 300,000 live chicks must be delivered to growing operations each week to replace them. To meet this demand, the entirety of McDonald County is devoted to raising chickens. Tyson and two other poultry companies effectively own the county. The local economy, unemployment rates, housing, water quality, and politics revolve around the poultry industry. Almost every aspect of county life is determined by decisions by Tyson, Inc., Simmons Foods, and MOARK/ Land O' Lakes Eggs. On any given day, McDonald County is home to 13 million chickens, plus a few hundred thousand turkeys. Those are large numbers but by themselves have little or no meaning. For the chicken destined to be included in tomorrow's eight-piece box, it means that life is nasty, brutish, and very short.

The chicks are incubated at a large hatchery and are delivered to a contract grower by the thousands. Consequently, there is no such thing as a chick; the creatures are simply viewed en masse. Typically, 22,000 chicks occupy one broiler house, but this number can vary from 11,000 to 30,000, depending on the size of the confinement building. Several hundred chicks of these thousands are crushed or suffocated or succumb to disease. Others are severely injured by handling during transfer to the large cardboard crates that transport them to the growing operation. Still others are injured upon transfer from the crates to the growing house. There is no attempt made to care for these diseased or injured chicks; they are considered just so much trash and are treated as such. The dying, diseased, or dead chicks are thrown into piles, using devices that can be operated without the need to stoop, and discarded.

The next six to seven weeks, depending on the company's schedule, the chicks spend in the confinement building. Every effort by the company and the grower goes toward making every chicken reach a weight of 2.5 to 5 lbs within that six-to-seven-week period. Aggressive chickens are debeaked to avoid injuries and cannibalism. Although efforts have been made to breed out this tendency in broilers, this aggressiveness is a genetic trait that persists in some birds. The feeds are specially formulated to ensure maximum growth at minimum cost. Antibiotics get added at subtherapeutic levels for efficient digestion of food and, allegedly, for disease prevention. Naturally, there is no attempt to treat a sick chicken—when a chicken gets ill, it is simply disposed of. Appetite enhancers, such as selenium and arsenic, are added to the feeds to force the chickens to keep eating. The climate is controlled. In winter months, large curtains are lowered to keep out the cold and retain the heat from the chickens' bodies; gas heaters are activated on extremely cold days. In summer, the curtains are raised to allow air flow. There are, however, no cooling devices. Fortunately, the climate of southwest Missouri is moderate, just as it is in other poultry-growing areas in the DelMarVa Peninsula, North Georgia, and central Texas. Few chickens are raised in far northern states or in desert areas.

Occasionally, however, weather disasters do strike. Excessive heat and humidity cause diminished appetites and high mortality rates. Heavy snowfall can cause the roofs of the shoddily constructed chicken houses to collapse. Long and severe cold snaps have the same effects as high heat and humidity: Chickens suffer. Southwest Missouri, northwest Arkansas, and northeast Oklahoma are subject to thunderstorms bringing high wind and even tornadoes that can devastate the vulnerable growing houses. Chickens become stressed or diseased. A catastrophic event can kill all chickens.

If all goes relatively well for the company and the grower, around 80 percent of the chicks will make it to the prescribed weight at the prescribed time. At this point, with what were two-ounce balls of down now weighing 2.5 to 5 pounds each, crowding becomes a very real problem. Twenty-two thousand chickens confined in a small space make things very difficult for the individual chicken. In addition to competition for food there is some cannibalism, even when the more aggressive birds have been debeaked. There is also an inevitable pecking order, meaning that less vigorous chickens lose feathers and then are pecked to bloody shreds since it is impossible for them to run or hide. Smothering becomes more and more prevalent as the chickens reach their full size. What was spacious for small chicks becomes overcrowded for seven-week-old chickens.

The torture comes to an end with the arrival of the catchers, crews sent out to catch the chickens and place them into crates. Catchers are hired by the trucking companies and normally don't have any of the benefits associated with full-time employment: no paid holidays, no health insurance, no vacations. Some are undocumented immigrants, almost all are from minority groups, and most are otherwise unemployable. These people are not, even on the best of days, in a position to be sensitive and caring individuals. After a few days or a few weeks on the job, even conscientious catchers become callous and indifferent to the suffering of individual chickens. Using wire devices that hook onto the chickens' legs or just grabbing handfuls of chickens by their legs, they toss and cram the birds into wooden crates until those crates are completely packed in. Some birds get injured, others are killed, but this doesn't matter; the next stop is the processing plant, where those not already dead will be killed.

The contract grower begins preparations for receiving the next delivery of chicks right after the chicken house is empty. The chicken-waste-laden dry litter, composed of whatever material is locally available—straw, ground corn cobs, rice hulls, peanut shells—is scooped out and spread onto fields adjacent to the growing houses, contributing to the contamination of local streams and rivers. The building is hosed and scrubbed down, then a new layer of litter laid down. All is ready for the next flock.

Meanwhile, the truck hauling the previous flock is barreling down the highway to the processing plant (which can be up to thirty-five miles away), feathers flying. In some parts of this country it is a common sight to view these trucks with chicken heads protruding from the crates, as if peering to see where they are going. In fact, ditches along some rural highways in southwest Missouri and northern Arkansas contain so many feathers that they look like snowdrifts. These chicken trains run all night and all day. The slaughterhouses process birds in two shifts. The day shifts and second shifts go from 8:00 A.M. to 11:00 P.M. The third or night shift is reserved exclusively for maintenance and to let the sanitation cleanup crews do their work.

Upon arrival at the slaughterhouse, the truck waits in line behind similar trucks, also laden with live or semilive chickens. In the summer, waiting trucks pull into sheds equipped with large fans to cool off the birds and to provide ventilation to prevent further mortality. In the cooler months, no such precautions are needed and the trucks simply wait in line.

Occasionally, a chicken manages to escape from the cages on the trucks. When I visited the Simmons slaughterhouse and packing plant in Southwest City, Missouri, I noted a lone chicken huddled in the parking lot. It was not moving, probably due to either confusion or injury. I remarked to the plant manager that the chicken ought to be rewarded for escaping. Instead, the suit-and-tie guy called to one of the drivers, who grabbed the escaped bird by the legs and walked away. It occurred to me later that the plant manager didn't see a living animal in distress; what he saw was a broiler.

The process of going from the receiving line to the disassembly line is straightforward. The crates of birds are un-loaded and each animal is paralyzed or stunned electrically (either by being dipped into a charged water bath or by insertion of an electric rod up the anus), then two slits are made in the jugular veins of its neck to bleed out as it is hung upside down on hooks on the line. This takes but a minute or so. After death, the carcass is scalded, then a mechanical whirring rubber "brush" removes the feathers, its entrails are removed, and other unwanted parts (beaks, wing tips) are sent to a protein plant, along with the feathers. These are rendered down to make pet foods and, grimly, chicken feed.

In processing 300,000 chickens per week, the slaughter-house discharges 800,000 gallons of wastewater per day. In the case of the Tyson slaughterhouse in Noel, Missouri, the waste-water goes into the Elk River. The Simmons slaughterhouse a few miles away discharges this amount into Cave Springs Branch, an otherwise dry stream. This wastewater contains blood, intestinal contents, fat, grease, and cleaning solvents.

On February 25, 1998, the Simmons plant was ordered closed by the Missouri Department of Natural Resources, after repeated violations of the Clean Water Act had resulted in the demise of all aquatic life in Cave Springs Branch. Simmons then upgraded its wastewater treatment plant. Upon the plant's resuming operations, what was termed an upset promptly occurred. Thousands of gallons of untreated or partially treated blood, grease, and chicken excrement got released into Cave Springs Branch. Downstream Oklahoman residents sued the company, and after an undisclosed settlement agreement in June of 2001 Simmons was allowed to continue operating.

After slaughtering, the birds are disassembled into component parts, chilled, and packed into boxes for shipping. Refrigerated trucks then haul the products to retail outlets. Tyson's trucks carry the company's oval logo and in large letters "Feeding You Like Family." Some contaminants from the intestinal contents and from the feathers in the whirring rubber brush remain on the chicken parts. Random testing of supermarket broilers and packaged portions has shown high levels of salmonella.

From the time the chick is hatched from an egg to the time when it bleeds to death hooked on the line, the animal is not treated as a sentient creature. The companies that raise and slaughter it consider it a unit of production, one among millions. The life of a broiler chicken is not a life, as we might define it. The chicken is a very small cog in the industrial machine.

Here are the top ten broiler companies rated by size according to 2003 figures and a summary of each company, taken from the companies' Web sites. Given that the poultry/broiler industry has led the way for the other animal industries, it is, I think, useful to summarize their operations. Appendix A contains this information in abbreviated form and lists the other broiler companies.

### THE TOP TEN BROILER COMPANIES

1. **Tyson Foods, Inc.,** with headquarters in Arkansas, produced 146 million pounds of prepared chicken meat between March 2001 and March 2002. The total number of chickens slaughtered in 2000 ex-

ceeded 2.2 billion, more than twice as many as the number-two producer, Gold Kist, Inc. Without doubt, Tyson is the biggest of the big. In 2000, prior to Tyson's acquiring its beef production unit (IBP), total sales were $23.8 billion. The company sells its product under its own brand name and markets its own products, though it also packages meats for supermarket brands. Tyson has 7,600 growers under contract with operations in sixteen states, though all are subject to the same contract provisioning. The company also has eighty-three processing plants in twenty states. These plants, according to Tyson's Web site, produce products ranging from Cornish game hens to boneless, skinless breast and from chicken patties to full dinners.

2. **Gold Kist, Inc.,** headquartered in Georgia, produced over 60 million pounds of prepared chicken between March 2001 and March 2002 and processed 7.2 million chickens, with annual sales totaling over $1.8 billion. Gold Kist started out as a small southern cooperative of thirteen cotton farmers in and around Carrollton, Georgia. The company expanded into feed and farm supply stores; the outlet in Gainesville, Georgia, began supplying broiler producers and opened a hatchery. Then it started contracting with broiler growers and constructing processing plants and distribution centers. In 1998, Gold Kist sold off its other operations and focused exclusively on poultry. It now has nine-

teen hatcheries, twelve feed mills, 2,500 contract growers, twelve slaughterhouse/processing plants, three by-product plants, and ten distribution centers. The products are sold mostly under its own brand, but as its Web site states, "Whether it's an elegant gourmet dinner, nuggets on a school lunch menu, or a bucket of chicken for a picnic, Gold Kist produces a variety of products to satisfy consumers' desires."

3. **Pilgrim's Pride, Inc.,** headquartered in Texas, produced 57 million pounds of processed chicken between March 2001 and March 2002. It also processed 300 million pounds of turkey and sold 50 million dozen eggs. Annual sales, including turkey and eggs, totaled $2.2 billion in 2001. Pilgrim's Pride began when Aubrey and Bo Pilgrim sold their first chicken behind their farm-supply store more than fifty years ago. They would give away 100 baby chicks with each feed sack purchase and then buy back the grown birds to sell at a profit. The demands for the chickens grew, and today Pilgrim's Pride is a modern, vertically integrated chicken company. Under the Pilgrim's Pride brand name, the retail line is sold regionally in the central, southwestern, and western United States. Bulk food service and industrial products are sold nationally and internationally as generic chicken and poultry parts. In 2001, the company acquired Wampler Foods (primarily turkeys) and increased

its capacity at processing plants in Nagadoches and Waco, Texas. Today the company has seven slaughterhouse processing plants, seven grow-out (company-owned growing operations) facilities, three value-added plants, and seven distribution centers and has sales and marketing divisions in Dallas, Texas, and Mexico City.

4. **ConAgra Poultry Companies** is part of a giant multinational company with far-reaching tentacles, with poultry operations headquartered in Georgia. The company is involved in various aspects of agribusiness, from production, to transportation, to processing and packaging, and has more than 80,000 employees worldwide. Its broiler operations processed 521 million birds in 2002. Annual sales of ConAgra's Poultry Division were over $2 billion. Poultry is sold primarily under the Peirce Chicken brand, but like the other major broiler companies, ConAgra also sells bulk products to food service and industrial companies. Some of ConAgra's other (besides chicken) brand-name products: Armour, Butterball, Eckrich, Healthy Choice, LambWeston, Meridian, Singleton, ConAgra Beef, Signature Meats, Hebrew National, Gebhardts, Hunt's, Van Camp's, Gilardi Foods, Banquet, Blue Bonnet, Parkay, Egg Beaters, Knott's Berry Farm, Swift Premium, Wesson, and many more. The company has eighteen slaughterhouse/packing plants that process over 10 million birds per week. No information

on hatcheries, feed mills, contract growers, or distribution centers is available on the Web site, but the company does claim to be a vertically integrated producer managing the quality process from egg to final product.

5. **Perdue Farms,** headquartered in Maryland, anticipated that 2003 production would be 48 million chickens and 4 million turkeys per week. Annual sales of $2.7 billion are reported. This company was founded in the 1920s by Arthur Perdue, who operated a table-egg poultry farm in Salisbury, Maryland, and is now the sixth-largest poultry production company in this country. In 1998, it entered into a joint venture agreement with a Chinese business to construct a poultry complex near Shanghai. Perdue relies upon 3,000 contract growers to supply the chickens for its processing plants. It describes itself as a vertically integrated agribusiness, operating hatcheries, feed mills, production and breeder operations, and processing/further processing plants. In addition to its poultry operations, the company is a NASCAR sponsor. Perdue markets its retail chicken products under its own brand name, Short Cuts, and Joan DeLuca, as well as other store brands. International brands are sold under names endemic to the marketed country. It has also invested in grains and oilseeds. In addition to the above information, which is on the company's Web site, in 2000, Perdue joined with

Missouri-based AgriRecycle to form Perdue AgriRecycle, LLC, a company that dries and converts poultry wastes to fertilizer pellets. This company was formed in response to assertions that chicken wastes were polluting the Chesapeake Bay. The company hopes to sell the pelletized fertilizer products to garden centers.

6. **Wayne Farms, LLC,** headquartered in Alabama, produced 27 million pounds of processed chicken between March 2001 and March 2002; the company has twelve processing plants in as many states. Little else can be found out about this company other than it claims to be vertically integrated, owning or managing all aspects of production, from feed mills, to distribution, to retail outlets. One reason for the dearth of information is that Wayne Farms is owned by ContiGroup Companies (CGC), a privately held international agribusiness specializing in integrated pork and poultry production, cattle feeding, and aquaculture, with nearly 200 years of experience in agribusiness and global trade. Luminaries such as Henry Kissinger sit on its board of directors. The company serves customers around the world through facilities and affiliates in ten countries. It operated as Continental Grain Company in the United States from 1921 to 1999, when it sold its commodity marketing operations and turned its principal focus to meat proteins. Founded in Belgium in 1813, it is one of the largest

privately held companies in the United States. However, since its stocks are not traded, no public reports are available and financial and systems information is very difficult to obtain. Wayne Farms was acquired by ContiGroup in 2000. Chicken products are sold under the Dutch Quality House brand.

7. **Sanderson Farms, Inc.,** headquartered in Mississippi, produced 22,830,000 pounds of processed chicken from March 2001 to March 2002. Total sales in fiscal year 2000 were $606 million. The company is "fully vertically integrated" and has over 600 contract growers, primarily in Mississippi and central Texas. According to its literature, the company started as a farm-supply business, owned by D. R. Sanderson Sr., which sold feed, seed, fertilizer, and other farm-related materials. After 1955, the company was incorporated by the senior Sanderson and his two sons and added poultry production, which has since become the primary focus. Chicken products are marketed under the Sanderson Farms' Miss Goldy brand. The company distributes its products in the Southeast, Southwest, Midwest, and West. It has six processing plants and one further processing plant. The plants are located in Collins, Hazlehurst, McComb, and Laurel, Mississippi; Hammond, Louisiana; and Bryan, Texas, with growing operations nearby the processing plants. Although not on their Web site,

Sanderson has been subjected to considerable criticism over its operations in the Navasota River area of central Texas where chicken wastes have been filtering into the Brazos River watershed. Over $500,000 was recently awarded to a quasi-governmental entity, the Brazos River Authority, to assist in cleaning up the watershed and keeping chicken wastes out.

8. **Cagle's, Inc.,** headquartered in Georgia, anticipated a total slaughter in 2003 of 26 million chickens. While somewhat difficult to calculate, total annual sales appear to be near $340 million. Cagle's started out as a storefront chicken shop in the heart of downtown Atlanta. Several years later, it purchased Strain Farms (described as a grow-out operation that grew chicks into broilers). In 1965, Cagle's built its own feed mill, then expanded into all aspects of fully integrated poultry production: breeder hens, hatcheries, contract growers, and slaughterhouse/processing plants (capable of processing 1.25 million chickens per week). The company Web site defines its vertical integration as follows: The company furnishes the chicks, feed, technical assistance, and any medications needed. The independent (*sic*) contractor farmers furnish facilities, labor, and the special care needed. Cagle's depends totally upon its contract growers to supply the chickens for "value-added processing" (also referred to as "further processing") that provides pre-

seasoned and ready-to-cook chickens and chicken parts. Selling retail under such house brands as Cagle's Pride IQF (IQF = Individually Quick Frozen) for bulk packaging and providing marinated and breaded parts for food service, the company primarily markets its products in the Southeast.

9. **Foster Farms,** headquartered in California, produced 20 million pounds of processed chicken from March 2001 to March 2002. The acquisition of Zacky Farms added 165 million pounds to this amount. No information was available on sales. Foster Farms is the largest West Coast producer of chickens, with operations primarily in California's Central Valley, but now is expanding into the southeastern United States. The company is vertically integrated but does not rely upon contract growers. Instead, it has its own "grow-out ranches" in California, Oregon, and Washington. While the company claims the feeds contain no steroids or growth hormones, it says nothing about using appetite enhancers. Nevertheless, the company claims that no antibiotics that are important for human medicine (tetracycline, penicillin, and sulfonomides) are administered to its animals. It also claims that it does not use fluoroquinolones (Cipro being one well-known brand) and also that all flocks are tested to ensure that antibiotics are not present before processing. Moreover, it asserts that its chickens are "grown in large poultry barns designed to protect

the birds from environmental extremes, while allowing natural light and fresh air . . . [and] adequate space for the birds to move freely. [T]he floors are covered with absorbent bedding materials such as rice hulls and wood shavings." Foster markets its products under its own brand names.

10. **Mountaire Farms, Inc.,** headquartered in Delaware, produced 18,620,000 pounds of processed chicken from March 2001 to March 2002. No information on numbers of chickens raised each year or on sales is available. It started out as a commercial feed business in Arkansas but since 1977 has focused on poultry production in the DelMarVa Peninsula and in North Carolina. The company describes itself as a leading vertically integrated poultry processor, servicing customers from coast to coast and internationally. It has three complexes: DelMarVa in Selbyville, Delaware; Mountaire Farms of North Carolina in Lumber Bridge; and Mountaire Farms of Delaware in Millsboro. Each complex produces retail, wholesale, and export chicken products and has its set of contract growers, but there is overlap between the two Delaware processing plants. Mountaire depends upon contract growers to supply live chickens to the processing plants. Yet while the company's Web site states that the company is looking for new growers, no information is available on the current number of growers or the

birds produced. Mountaire Farms markets its products to retail outlets and supermarkets, which then put their own label on Mountaire products. The company does market one product—Sizzlin Sensations, "a restaurant-quality chicken meal ready to eat in only 10 minutes."

While Tyson is by far the largest, the others are constantly jockeying for position, so the preceding rankings may not reflect current production. But, all forty-two of the biggest companies operate in a manner similar to Tyson. Some may own all their own facilities and operate without contract growers, others may operate only with contract growers, but most, including Tyson, have some mix of the two.

There is one common element however: They are all completely vertically operated. They own, manage, or control it all, from semen to cellophane. Yet most of the companies, the exceptions being the ones owned by the multinationals (ContiGroup, ConAgra), highlight their humble beginnings. Only forty-two companies engaged in broiler production are responsible for over 95 percent of the chickens produced for meat in this country. No more humble beginnings are allowed.

## THE NATIONAL ORGANIZATIONS

Following internal struggles in the mid-1990s among various organizations representing poultry producers, these groups put aside their differences and united under the banner of the National Poultry and Egg Association. NPEA serves as the educational, marketing, grant-making, and scholarship wing of the poultry industry.

The National Broiler Council and the National Poultry Federation are the political and lobbying wings of the poultry industry. Headquartered in Washington, D.C., among other functions these serve to represent the interests of poultry and egg producers to Congress and to the various agencies (USDA, FDA, EPA) that exercise control over the industry. There are boards of directors, elected by the membership, and the national boards set policy and direct the activities of the staffs.

The relationship between Don Tyson and Pres. Bill Clinton is a larger-than-life example of the political influence of Big Chicken. Mike Espy, initially secretary of agriculture, got caught in the fallout from this relationship and was forced to resign, although he was eventually cleared of the charges. Recently poultry growers, through the preceding lobbying organizations, achieved a twofold victory in Washington. Through their efforts, livestock operations, including poultry, were exempted from the Clean Air Act, in a proposed regulation by the EPA touted as a "safe harbor" for agricultural facilities, and they pressured Congress into opening up 2002 Farm Bill funding for large CAFOs. The latter move had been rejected by Congress in 1996, and President Clinton's second secretary of agriculture, Dan Glickman, further resisted such efforts.

## Big Egg

Charlie and Marge had worked hard to buy a few acres and a house in the country. Charlie still works at a chicken hatchery over by Pineville, Missouri. Marge retired after years of working for the county public works department. After investing their life's savings in the house and five acres, they were set to settle down and enjoy their waning years. They'd be the first to admit that their modest two-bedroom cottage home and small plot was not exactly as envisioned in the "American Dream," but it was their dream. It had everything they wanted: a vegetable and flower garden, a nice grassy lawn, and a front porch with a swing. There was a flagpole in the front yard. The living room walls are covered with photos of their children and grandchildren—all of whom live elsewhere. As Charlie states bluntly, "Hell, there ain't nothing to keep them here. Just chickens and a packing plant. Minimum wages. No future in it." Marge collects Beanie Babies, housed in a cabinet Charlie built for them.

In the evenings, after the Channel 12 news, Charlie and Marge used to sit in the swing on the front porch and watch the fireflies—"lightnin' bugs"—rising from the garden and yard. But at some point the foul reek drifting with the breezes on warm, humid nights got so bad they went inside and closed the windows. Foul odors were nothing new. After all, they lived in Missouri's "chicken country," where there are massive broiler houses and egg-laying operations aplenty. But this was different. It was the smell of death and decay.

"It smelled really bad—like what you smell sometimes when you pass a dead, bloated roadkill deer on the highway," says Charlie, whose house was unfortunately located just east, or downwind, of the source of the smell. "We've kinda gotten used to the chicken shit smell—that's around most of the time and we just live with it. But this was really bad—to the point of gagging."

Charlie and Marge called the county health officials, they called the Missouri Department of Health, they called the Missouri Department of Natural Resources, and they even called the State Highway Patrol. They put in calls to every local and state agency that they thought might come out and investigate. But no agency would take responsibility, each pointing to one of the others. Finally, Charlie and Marge gave up, turned on an air conditioner they had bought, and closed their doors and windows. Eventually the foul reek diminished and finally disappeared altogether. Months later they learned that the source of the stink was the dead and decaying bodies of the thousands of laying hens that had been abandoned.

Just down the road from Charlie and Marge adjacent to one of the world's largest egg-laying sites (then Vaughn Brothers, now MOARK/Land O' Lakes; MOARK is just a name, not an acronym for anything), tank trucks spread the wastes from the laying-house pits literally into the yard and garden of Jack and Nancy. Their house and yard are almost a copy of the one owned by Charlie and Marge: "The field next door belonged to the Vaughn Brothers and they would use it to spread the chicken crap from the buildings. That was pretty bad; it's just to the west of our yard. It got to where we couldn't hardly go outside, and we just stayed inside while they were spreading and for several days afterwards. But, I come home from work one day, I work up in Joplin, and here was all this stuff on my yard and in the garden. And it wasn't just chicken crap, although that would have been bad enough. There were also chicken bones, feathers, broken eggs, you name it. What they had done was drive the truck right along the fence between our property and theirs—and half the stuff went on their land and half on ours.

"Here's how it works: They pump the waste out of pits at the ends of the buildings and into these tanker trucks, just like the ones that put oil down for chip-and-seal on county roads. They have these slingers, sort of like sideways propellers, on the back of the trucks. They open a valve, the stuff pours down on the spinning slingers, and the gunk is spread out over the field. Except that, in this case, it got spread out over my yard and garden."

Jack and Nancy thought about suing. But Nancy's cousin worked for Vaughn Brothers, Inc., and they feared that she would lose her job if they brought suit. So while they got an attorney and met with other neighbors who had been subjected to similar incidents, they never filed a lawsuit. They also contacted conservation and sustainable agriculture groups. However, since Jack and Nancy were unwilling to file a complaint, no one could help them. Several years later, tired, depressed, and beaten down, they quietly sold out and moved away. The egg-laying company is still using the same methods of disposing of the wastes from the buildings.

McDonald County, Missouri, is the somewhat wretched "home," if that's the right word, to 13 million broiler chickens and a few hundred thousand turkeys. Their waste is more than enough to make the rivers run full of "nutrients from livestock operations," in the euphemism of the Missouri Department of Natural Resources. Every stream in McDonald County is on the "impaired waterbody" list for not meeting minimum water quality standards. The streams fill up in the summer with algae, which dies and rots in the fall. In water, decay uses oxygen and gives off carbon dioxide. Oxygen levels fall to a point where fish can't survive. As local fishermen complain, "there ain't nothing to catch."

As if this weren't enough, injury has been added to insult, just west of the hamlet of Anderson, Missouri. MOARK/Land O' Lakes' massive egg-laying operation dominates the landscape. Housing over 1 million laying hens, this facility embraces all the modern integration: an on-site feed mill that grinds and mixes the feed ingredients and the antibiotics, an egg-laying building (more on that shortly), and a processing plant where the eggs are washed, candled, and packaged. Its neighbors have complained about fine particles of dust from the feed mill that coat everything and about the stink from the blackish waste spread on nearby fields. The Missouri Department of Natural Resources responded and issued Notices of Violation (NOVs) of the Clean Air Act. There have been no fines or penalties, and, subsequently, nothing has changed.

The MOARK/Land O' Lakes' McDonald County site operational system (the company also owns operations in Colorado and California) is similar to that of egg-laying operations throughout the country. And as with other livestock operations that employ a "wet-handling" manure system, the common complaint from neighbors involves odor. The smell of chicken waste wafts for miles across the rolling green hills of McDonald County, a sweet, sickening odor considered normal. When the egg-laying company cleans out the pits, transfers the wastes to tanker trucks, and applies the black gunk to the fields, the area reeks.

Although the chicken wastes are supposedly used as fertilizer at "agronomic rates," there are parts of the application lands where no plants will grow. Chicken excrement is, among other things, high in ammonia and phosphorous. Applied overzealously by the tank truck drivers, it will cause the fescue and other grasses to become "burned out." The plants first turn yellow, then die.

Farmers in the area have signed spreading agreements with MOARK/Land O' Lakes and the previously discussed broiler operations. These agreements allow the chicken companies to spread the cesspit contents and the broiler litter to the farmers' fields. According to one farmer, "Well, it seemed like a good deal at the time. They would pay for everything, give me free fertilizer, it would cut way down on my costs, so I signed their agreement. It hasn't turned out quite so rosy—they put that junk on so thick that it completely smothers out the fescue or alfalfa or whatever I was growing there. If anything survives that, the nitrogen content in the chicken crap is so high that it just burns out large areas. The best thing that can happen is to get a hard rain right after they put it on, so it'll get washed off. Of course, then it ends up in Patterson Creek, and that's not so good.

"But the worst thing is, they bring it out when they're ready to do so. The agreement I signed doesn't even require them to call me and let me know. If their pits get full, I get shit all over the place whether it is needed or not. And now, damned if I didn't find out that this amounts to a permanent easement. They went down and placed a copy of this on my deed, so that this agreement is passed down if I wanted to sell this place or one of my boys gets it when I die. That little agreement I signed—well, it wasn't so little."

Though the Missouri Department of Natural Resources and the EPA are both aware that the poultry operations are responsible for the pollution that has caused the impairment, to use their term, of all streams in the county, the agencies have shown no inclination to require the laying houses to change their waste-handling practices. Instead, the EPA appointed a "working group" consisting primarily of representatives of the industries that are causing the problem, no one representing the interests of the local farmers and rural residents. Little of significance is expected to come from this group to address the pollution in the streams of McDonald County or the Elk River, which flows through McDonald County on its way to the Grand Lake of the Cherokees in Oklahoma.

However, one development occurred when the federal and state agencies used DNA testing on the manure runoff to locate its source. They tested cow manure to establish one of the baselines, and then that cow manure contained DNA from chickens. What was happening was that the cows had eaten fescue on which chicken litter had been applied and thus also eaten the chicken shit, leading to the false readings on the DNA tests. New tests were developed that corrected this problem. Some local wags wrote some new lyrics to that old Waylon Jennings/Willie Nelson song: "Mommas, don't let your cows grow up to eat chicken shit."

### A LAYING CHICKEN'S LIFE

Photos showing laying hens crammed into tiny cages have regularly appeared in publications put out by the Animal Welfare Institute, People for the Ethical Treatment of Animals, and Farm Sanctuary. They depict the reality of modern egg production, which almost defies description.

Up to ten hens are put in cages no larger than five feet by five feet. A hen normally begins laying eggs at twelve to sixteen weeks of age and continues laying for around sixty weeks. Most hens are "spent" before they reach two years of age and are sold to make chicken soup and other processed foods in which the meat can be made tender through cooking. Some of the toughest meat is used in pet food. (However, when the market for these products is glutted, the spent hens may simply be killed. What is done with the carcasses is a matter of some conjecture; some are thought to be fed back to the living chickens or mixed in with hog feeds. There have been experiments with composting, with mixed success, as there is little market for the results.)

The cages are tilted slightly, so that the eggs can roll gently down into a catch tray to be collected by a conveyor belt that transports the eggs to the processing plant. With less modern or older systems, the eggs are collected manually. The cages are stacked four to six high, usually in pyramid fashion. These are covered with a metal roof, to keep the excrement and other wastes (broken eggs, feathers) from the cages above from going into the lower cages. Water flows over the roofs, carrying the wastes down into a central pit. Large chain-driven paddles push the more solid wastes into a large holding cesspit located at the end of each building. It is then pumped into tank trucks, which carry it to and spread it on adjacent fields.

The hens spend their entire lives in these tiny cages; their feet and claws sometimes become distorted from being bent around the wires of their cage. As gruesome as this is, those concerned about the humane treatment of farm animals find two practices by the egg-laying companies particularly atrocious, neither of which are used by sustainable free-range poultry operations: debeaking and forced molting.

Debeaking means exactly what it says: The chicken's beak is clipped, chiefly to prevent the hens from pecking one another. While there is some debate over whether correct debeaking causes the animal pain, there is no such debate that debeaking well beyond the tip does. Chickens that have been subjected to such improper debeaking become traumatized due to long-term pain and have proven to be less productive than chickens that either have not been debeaked or had only the beak tip removed. Chickens are cannibalistic by nature, and while this trait seems more or less to have been bred out of broiler chickens, such is not the case with laying hens. It is likely that the overcrowding system used by the industry causes stress, which leads to extreme cannibalism. Rather than convert to a less stressful system, the egg companies choose to debeak the chickens, adding further stress—another Catch-22 situation.

Forced molting requires a bit of explanation. Molting means a periodic losing of feathers, a natural occurrence in all birds. With a laying hen, molting naturally occurs when she reaches an age of about eighteen to twenty months and egg production ceases until this process is completed—that is, the feathers grow back, after a few months. Some flocks are sold for slaughter at this point, and a replacement flock takes their place. However, such replacement is costly, so the ever-resourceful university and egg company researchers have determined that after two periods of "controlled" or forced molts, one at fourteen months and another at twenty-two months, and after a rest period of four to eight weeks after each molt, egg production and quality is much more consistent than with a "natural" molt at eighteen to twenty months.

The forced molt involves removal of all feeds until the

chicken loses between 25 and 35 percent of her body weight. The weight loss causes hormones to kick in and the chicken to enter a molt. There are also unintended consequences, however: The chicken's bones become fragile and break, and she can die. Moreover, the eggs from chickens that have been force-molted are far more likely to be contaminated.

## THE INCREDIBLE, INEDIBLE EGG

MOARK's McDonald County site also contains egg-washing facilities. In the process of being laid, then rolling down the cage and getting transported along the conveyor belt, the eggs pick up litter, debris, albumin, and excrement. Before eggs are packaged and crated, the material sticking to their shells must be removed. In the first quarter of 2003, MOARK/Land O' Lakes sold 202 million dozen eggs; that's 2.4 billion eggs requiring a lot of washing and resulting in a lot of stuff going down the drain. In the washing process, a few eggs get broken, and even a few out of 2.4 billion adds up rather quickly, and MOARK/Land O' Lakes is just one company of many. Buckeye Egg in Ohio, which was operating under an appeal of a closure order, confined 15 million laying hens, each producing at least one egg per day. The operation has since been sold.

So, other than polluting, stink, dead hens, debeaking, forced molting, broken eggs, and contaminated washwater to annoy the neighbors (and those downwind and downstream), what's the problem? There is, in fact, an enormous consumer problem. While egg producers like to brag about the "incredible, edible egg," the facts are likewise incredible: The CDC estimate that 1 out of every 10,000 eggs is contaminated with salmonella. Given the number of eggs sold and consumed in this country (in 2002 that number was 86.7 billion), the odds that contaminated eggs will end up in the grocery store are quite high. And the odds that someone will have a gastrointestinal upset or worse from *Salmonella enteriditis* is likewise high. Any cracking or breaking of the eggshell will add to the likelihood of contamination. When 86.7 billion eggs are processed (washed, candled, packaged) each year, if only 1 percent have cracked shells, over 8 million eggs are subject to contamination resulting from fecal matter coming into contact with the contents of the egg through the crack(s).

In response to the threats of a *Salmonella enteriditis* outbreak and in general response to scandals involving the health and safety of eggs, the Food and Drug Administration, along with industry groups, is, as it phrases it, "fighting back" by attempting to place the responsibility for safe consumption of eggs on the consumer. The FDA is advising consumers:

1. Don't eat raw eggs.

2. Buy eggs only sold in the grocer's refrigerated case.

3. Open the carton and check that the eggs are clean and uncracked.

4. Store eggs in the coldest part of the refrigerator (at forty degrees centigrade or below)

5. Keep hard-cooked eggs (such as Easter eggs) in the refrigerator and use within one week.

6. Don't freeze eggs in their shells.

7. Wash hands, utensils, equipment, and work areas with warm soapy water before and after contact with eggs and egg-rich foods.

8. Don't leave cooked eggs out of the refrigerator for more than two hours.

9. Cook eggs until the yolks are firm.

Number three is the most obvious example of an attempt to make the consumer responsible for improper sanitary procedures by the egg producer and processing plant. Eggs should never be packaged in an unclean state, and cracked or broken eggs should not be placed in a carton. It is true that rough handling during transport may cause eggshells to crack—but if one egg is so damaged, it is likely that the entire carton of eggs is likewise damaged. The industrial methods used by egg-laying facilities process hundreds of thousands of eggs per day. With a system that places high value on speed and efficiency, it is inevitable that unclean and cracked eggs get placed in cartons. However, it should not be the responsibility of consumers to ensure that eggs they buy are safe enough to eat. We are long past the era of *caveat emptor*, "buyer beware," and the FDA and the USDA need to place the responsibility for safe egg consumption exactly where it belongs: on the industry that produces such unsafe products. Making the consumer accountable may be a goal of the egg industry, but this should not be the goal of the agencies whose job is to ensure food safety.

## ROTTEN EGG-LAYING OPERATIONS

The aforementioned Buckeye Egg Farm operation in Ohio, formerly owned and operated by Anton Pohlmann, housed around 15 million laying hens. In 2000, a tornado wiped out twelve of the laying houses, immediately destroying up to a million chickens. Unaccustomed to freedom, thousands of other chickens wandered aimlessly inside and around the devastated confinement buildings. Eventually, the devastated chicken buildings and the contents were bulldozed and covered with dirt. Apparently, hundreds of thousands of chickens were buried alive.

Since the operation opened in 1980, those living nearby have complained of odor, fouled waters, and a plague of flies; when Buckeye expanded in 1995, complaints accelerated. The Ohio Department of Agriculture and the Ohio Department of Environmental Quality dutifully inspected and issued several NOVs, which the Buckeye Egg operation routinely ignored.

Local newspapers chronicled the plight of those living nearby. An article in the *Cincinnati Enquirer* December 10, 1999, read:

> Robert Bear and his wife Rosella used to host the Bear family reunion each summer. But that was before the Buckeye Egg Farm cranked up its operation across the road from his Wyandot County farm in the mid-1990s.
>
> "In 1998, I had to put plastic over all of the tables to keep the flies off," Rosella said. "We had it one more year, and then we had to quit."

Dan Perkins, 75, said he didn't get to watch his grandsons ride the tractors on his Licking County farm this year.

"They wouldn't come out anymore," said Perkins, whose property borders a Buckeye Egg farm. "This year, the flies were the worst they have ever been. I've put out all kinds of traps and fly strips, thinking I could stop them there, but they covered the garage."

Buckeye Egg, the state's largest egg-producing operation with 115 barns and 15 million chickens, has earned a national reputation—for environmental irresponsibility.

Since Germany native Anton Pohlmann bought 2,300 acres of central Ohio farmland in 1978, the giant egg business has angered neighbors, activists and state officials by repeatedly flouting the state's environmental laws.

Karen Davis, president of United Poultry Concerns, a consumer advocacy organization, wrote on May 3, 2002, to the *Columbus Dispatch*. What she wrote bears reproducing in full:

**Factory Farms' Ethical Problems All Too Real**
*Thanks to The Dispatch for its April 23 editorial*
*"State Crackdown."*

As well as the farm's atrocious environmental record, the editorial noted that Germany twice convicted Buckeye Egg's owner, Anton Pohlmann, of cruelty to animals for abuse of the company's hens. Germany is way ahead of the United States in its protection of egg-producing hens.

The National Public Radio show *Living on Earth* aired a

report April 19 [2002] on Germany's decision to ban cages for laying hens by 2012. Caged hens, according to the European Scientific Veterinary Committee, "suffer intensely and continuously."

While addressing the environmental issues, we need to consider the husbandry from which factory farms' environmental mess is flowing. Buckeye Egg Farm exhibits the link between the way hens are being forced to live and the pollution that people are increasingly experiencing as a result.

Under the new German law, farmers will not be permitted to house more than 6,000 hens together in one building. This measure alone will benefit hens and the environment at the same time.

It's deplorable that children are fighting off flies at school, but the hens in cages have no escape from those same flies buzzing in their eyes and spawning maggots in the corpses beside them. In short, there's an ethical problem as well as an environmental problem that demands our attention.

Finally, however, after a series of newspaper articles, an aggressive campaign by Ohio's sustainable agriculture, environmental, and conservation organizations, and because of pressure from national organizations, the state and federal agencies could no longer just issue NOVs without enforcing them. After a "cease and desist" order regarding the flies and odor was repeatedly violated, the Ohio secretary of agriculture ordered the operation to close. Buckeye remained open, still operating, still polluting, and still stinking out the neighbors, until 2004, which is when the secretary of agriculture ordered complete closure. Buckeye appealed the closure order but then sold the operation to another agribusiness. But at least the Ohio secretary of agriculture responded, unlike the situation in other states where state regulatory agencies ignore violation after violation, where enforcement of clean water, clean air, and nuisance laws never occurs, and where companies are issued renewed permits regardless of past or present sins. It is unusual for state and federal environmental protection agencies to take action against the large egg-producing companies. It is even more unusual for the USDA and FDA to do so, as they remain inclined to place the onus for disease prevention on consumers and have been for quite some time. The CDC note that eggs are one of the primary sources of food-borne illnesses, as evidenced by this statement issued in 1988:

A total of 6390 SE isolates were reported for 1987 (16% of total reported Salmonella isolates). SE [*Salmonella enteriditis*] is the second most common Salmonella serotype reported. National surveillance data for 1987 indicate continued high isolation rates of SE in the northeast, mid-Atlantic, and south Atlantic regions . . . Of the 19 outbreaks caused by SE with a known vehicle reported to CDC in 1987, 15 (79%) were associated with Grade A shell eggs. No vehicle of transmission was known for 11 other reported outbreaks of SE infections in 1987.

Although food handling errors can contribute to outbreaks of Salmonella infections, the outbreaks in Fort Monmouth, New Jersey (ice cream), and Livonia, New York (egg omelet), demonstrate that SE infections can occur even when acceptable food preparation techniques have been used.

Long-term control of SE may depend on the elimination of infected flocks or use of pasteurized egg products. Proper handling and cooking of eggs can minimize the risk of salmonellosis (2); thorough cooking kills Salmonella.

Clinicians are encouraged—but not required—to report cases of salmonellosis to local and state health departments. Salmonella isolates can be serotyped by most state public health laboratories to aid in epidemiologic investigations.

This CDC statement notes that "even when acceptable food preparation techniques have been used" *Salmonella enteriditis* infections can occur. Clearly, asking consumers to ensure proper preparation of eggs and egg dishes will not change matters. Even when they take every possible precaution, consumers cannot make the egg free of food-borne illnesses. State and federal agencies must ensure that eggs are free from contamination upon leaving the processing plants. It is relatively easy to identify and remove chickens whose innards are infected with salmonella. This may result in a short-term reduction of the flock, but it would mean that the burden for ensuring pathogen-free eggs is placed where it belongs: on the companies that are in the business of eggs. Instead of "buyer beware" it should be "seller beware." This is not likely to happen. As has been detailed, when agribusiness companies control every aspect of egg production, from the feed mills to retail packaging, it is to their benefit to externalize as many costs as possible. That means they benefit and everyone else loses.

# BIG MILK

AT THE TULS DAIRY IN SOUTH-CENTRAL IDAHO'S MAGIC Valley, a thousand or so cows lined up for their twice-daily milking; another thousand cows were taking in feed and water from the concrete troughs. Tanker trucks were backed up to haul the raw milk to the cheese-processing plants in Jerome. Meanwhile, workers at the huge dairy were burying "downed" cows, burying them alive, that is. Unfortunately, probably not an atypical day at one of this country's megadairies.

One thing that was different is that Idaho's TV, radio, and newspaper reporters had been tipped off that one or more cows had been buried alive and were reporting the news. The Idaho State Department of Agriculture, nominally in charge of overseeing dairy practices, investigated after complaints came rolling in from rural residents in the area of the dairy and it had seen photos that caused hardened reporters to avert their eyes. The ISDA investigator then took more photos, which were examined by veterinarians at ISDA, and the conclusion was indeed that at least one downer cow had been buried alive and several others had not received even basic care, including food and water. They were just dragged out into an open lot next to the burial pit and left to die, slowly and excruciatingly.

This was too much, even for the ISDA, normally an advocate for industrial dairies. It took an unprecedented action and filed "animal abuse" charges, as well as fining the dairy $5000.00. At first, the county attorney declined to file charges against Jack Tuls, the owner of the dairy, maintaining that there was no evidence that Mr. Tuls was aware of this abuse and therefore he could not be held legally accountable. Then a dairy employee came forward and stated that not only was Jack Tuls aware of what was going on, but he had also, in fact, ordered it. The Twin Falls County prosecuting attorney filed charges.

As of this writing, the case was postponed at the request of the defendant. Tuls sold his interest in the dairy and is now listed as "former owner." He also publicly acknowledged that chronic and excessive alcohol consumption was at the base of his problems.

In a later episode that embarrassed the leadership of the Idaho Dairy Association, a state legislator who was also a dairyman defended the practice of dragging live but downed cows around with a tractor. In testimony before a committee of the Idaho General Assembly, concerning a bill that would strengthen and clarify the state law on animal abuse, this legislator/dairyman maintained that it was often necessary to attach chains or ropes to live cows and drag them, for example, out of a ditch. What he said appalled fellow ranchers and farmers. "My God, man," they replied, "at least put a bullet in their head before dragging them around."

Jack Tuls first established his dairy in the Magic Valley after the California Regional Water Quality Board issued orders prohibiting "waste disposal" in the Chino Valley, where Tuls had previously owned a dairy. Specifically, these were "cease and desist" orders (numbers 99–11 and 99–65) stating: "Disposal of manure to land is prohibited, unless allowed by separate water discharge requirements issued by the Board . . ." These orders were issued to the Tuls operation, as well as to all other dairies in this "agricultural zone," because the groundwater in the area had become polluted by "salts" after years of waste disposal by industrial dairies. Rather than haul the dairy waste out of the Chino Basin, a costly alternative to on-site disposal, Tuls and others had gone looking for "inviting locations" where few or no restrictions were imposed on their operations. They found them in such places as the Magic Valley of Idaho; in Erath County, Texas; the Yakima/Sunnyside area of Washington; and in and around Clovis, New Mexico. These areas welcomed the dairies, and the state agencies in charge of air emission and water discharge issued permits on a first-come, first-served basis. In some locales no permits were required at all.

Very few regulations or laws existed to govern dairies in traditional livestock-raising areas. And, as it turned out, these dairies were anything but traditional. The state agencies were ill-equipped to impose any restrictions.

Most of the dairy owners were of Dutch heritage, and in the areas cited earlier they became known as the "Dutch

Dairy Mafia." Indeed, it appears that the owners of the dairies that left the Chino Basin established operations in at least two of the regions noted earlier. A comparison of the owners' names in Erath County, Texas, for example, reveals that these names match closely the names of the owners in Idaho's Magic Valley and those in Clovis, New Mexico, and Yakima/Sunnyside, Washington. Tuls, for example appears as the name of the registered owner of dairies in Texas and Nebraska, in addition to the one in Magic Valley. The DeRuyter family owns dairies in Washington State near Sunnyside, Pasco, and Outlook, near Marsing, Idaho, and near Mesquite, New Mexico, and previously owned the dairy in the Chino Basin.

The owners claim that they established these operations where they did because of access to markets, and there is some truth to this. Erath County, Texas, is relatively close to the Dallas–Fort Worth metroplex, and Yakima/Sunnyside is a short drive from both Portland and Seattle. There is no apparent market reason for any dairies to exist in Curry County, New Mexico, or in the Snake River Plains of Idaho: There is no ready access to nearby markets there. Yet these operations continue to grow. Now cheese plants have followed the milk. Most of the milk produced in the Magic Valley is sold to Jerome Cheese, which appears to have some sort of contractual or proprietary relationship to the Kraft Company. The dairies in and around Twin Falls, Filer, Buhl, Hagerman, Jerome, and Bliss, all situated in the Magic Valley, do not produce milk for direct human consumption. One reason may be that the dairies do not need to meet such exacting health and sanitary standards for any milk produced that will be further-processed for cheeses.

Another, more compelling reason is that the cheese plants will take all the milk that industrial dairies can produce. Glanbia Cheese, for example, announced in the summer of 2003 that it was seeking to construct a new cheese plant in either eastern New Mexico or the Texas Panhandle, due to the fact that the "dairies are already there." There are a number of former Chino Basin dairies in eastern New Mexico, centered around Clovis in Curry County, but only one such operation in the Panhandle region of Texas. The company recently announced that the new cheese plant would be located in or near Clovis, New Mexico, having rejected an option to locate the facility in Cassia County, Idaho, as no dairy industry existed in that county.

Cheese plants require a lot of water, and it is uncertain where Glanbia will get this in Curry County, New Mexico. Clovis is the county seat, located on the southern edge of what is known as the Ogallala Aquifer. This aquifer is fast being depleted. The state engineer of New Mexico estimated that the Ogallala Aquifer in Curry County would no longer exist by 2010. The city council of Clovis and the Curry County commission are scrambling to find substitute sources and are trying to secure a federal grant to bring water from the Ute Reservoir, almost 100 miles away. Not only is the federal bailout uncertain, but also the Ute Reservoir is both almost dry and on the "impaired waterbodies" roster, the list of heavily polluted waters compiled by the EPA. It seems very unlikely that the federal government would invest millions of dollars on a pipeline from a lake containing heavily polluted water—and not much of even that.

Like the other livestock industries, the dairy industry has

been both growing and diminishing. The average herd size has increased, while the number of dairy farmers has decreased. State agriculture departments and the USDA claim not to have any data on the number of dairy farmers; nonetheless, the decline in numbers is relatively easy to calculate. Given that the average herd size nationwide has increased from 100 to 850, it may be assumed that for every farmer who milked 100 cows, one farmer now milks 850 cows and that therefore the number of dairy farmers has decreased by 80 percent over the past decade. There are notable exceptions: The herd size and the number of dairy farmers in Wisconsin, the self-proclaimed Dairy State, has remained fairly constant, due, it seems, to rigid regulations on larger herds. On the other side of things, the average herd size in California now approaches 1,000 cows, up from only 250 or so in the early 1990s.

## How Milk Became Part of Our Diet

Milk was not a traditional staple in this or any other country until pasteurization was developed. The process was discovered inadvertently by Louis Pasteur when he found that holding milk at a high temperature, just below boiling, for a few minutes killed all bacteria. This changed everything. Until then, milk could not be kept for more than a few days. Bacteria caused the product to spoil quickly: Milk was a major contributor to all sorts of gastrointestinal distress. But with pasteurization came a product that could be maintained without danger of spoiling for several weeks. This brought an end to food-borne illnesses being caused by raw milk. There have been, however, outbreaks of illnesses caused by improper pasteurization, despite the fact that dairies and milk-processing plants rely upon relatively rigid formulas. The basic formula is the higher the temperature achieved, the shorter the time necessary. Glitches in the pasteurization process at a few processing plants resulted in contaminated milk getting delivered to consumers. But, all in all, this process works and has been key in the development of the milk industry.

Initially, pasteurization was opposed by those who claimed it gave milk a "cooked" taste and destroyed vitamins and nutritional values. The dairy industry, and its lobbyists, responded with a campaign to make milk products a basic element in the diet. The degree of their success can be best understood by supermarkets' practice of placing dairy products (milk, cheese, yogurt, butter) at the far reaches of the store—ensuring that shoppers must pass all other items on the way to access the dairy case. Another key element has been government largesse, brought about in part due to lobbying efforts of the dairy industry, which has become one of the most influential forces in the halls of Congress. The subsidies for milk are colossal, and while the subsidization calculus is complex, it essentially guarantees that dairy owners will make a profit, by establishing a standard similar to parity, which is based on the USDA's calculation of the break-even point for dairy owners. If the market price falls below that standard, the producer receives a check for the deficit from Uncle Sam.

The result is similar to what happens with other government-supported agriculture: Overproduction is rewarded. The larger the herd, the more overproduction and the bigger the government check. Overproduction leads to a market glut, leading to price declines and further compensation for "losses." The

Freedom to Farm bill was designed to end this giveaway. It was passed in 1996, by which point even those government officials either trained or paid to look the other way could not ignore the disastrous and unintended consequences of subsidies. But after a heavy lobbying effort by the dairy industry, first Congress extended the price support program and then the 2002 Farm Bill, signed into law by President Bush, made the prop-up program permanent.

Two factors, control of pathogens through pasteurization and a seemingly endless supply of government monies, have led to a surfeit of milk. There is simply no market demand for milk at the current levels of production. Yet, thanks to the welfare system initiated and maintained by Congress, the dairy industry is immune to the vagaries of the free market. The subsidies have been bitterly contested by agricultural and trade agencies in European and other countries, which claim that this program artificially supports the American dairy industry and violates free trade agreements. Subsidies afforded European dairies by the European Union, although in lesser amounts than their American counterparts, have been subjected to similar criticism from African and other developing nations.

As this is written, 1.3 billion pounds of surplus milk in powdered form is stored in temperature- and humidity-controlled caves. These caves are actually inactive limestone quarries located throughout the country, with most in and around Kansas City, Missouri. According to workers at the Kansas City storage area, about 20 to 25 million pounds of nonfat powdered dry milk arrive each week. "They keep making it, and we keep buying it," said Steve Gill, a spokesman for the USDA. "They" are the dairies that get paid regardless of supply and demand and "we," of course, are all of us taxpayers. "They" have over-produced 386 million pounds between October of 2002 and June of 2003, and it keeps coming in, filling up the caves. Storage costs for the powdered milk reached $20 million per year. Even with the temperature and humidity controls, dry milk cannot be stored for longer than three years. Some gets donated for domestic use and for foreign consumption; the remainder is destroyed. During the prolonged drought in the West in 2003 the U.S. secretary of agriculture, Anne Venneman, directed that surplus powdered milk be provided free of charge to livestock producers in drought-stricken counties. The problem is that powdered milk must be reconstituted with water to be used. Moreover, there is a vicious cycle at work here: The government provides subsidies to dairies for over-production, then provides the surplus as a feed supplement to the producers that have caused the surplus in the first place. Foreign governments, rural residents, and local farmers decry this USDA (tagged the U.S. Dairy Association by anti-megadairy activists) support of the dairy industry.

However, it is pollution, including stifling odors, flies, and overapplication of manure leading to fouling of streams, and mistreatment of the cows that spawn the most objections. Over a thousand complaints of the dairies' foul odors have been filed with the ISDA (which has declared such smells "normal agricultural odors," despite the recent advent of the huge dairies). The Texas cities of Belton, Waco, Killeen, and Temple have filed a joint complaint against the Texas Commission of Environmental Quality and the dairies in Erath County for contaminating their water supplies (in the watersheds of the Leon and Bosque Rivers, which originate in and flow through the waste-application areas). Flies have reached a pestilence stage in Idaho's Magic Valley and in Curry County, New Mexico. Cesspit wastes have overflowed roads and polluted local trout streams in south-central Idaho (Salmon Valley Creek, for example) after overzealous application of manure and urine to fields around the dairies. Catastrophic failures of lagoons have led to complete contamination of streams in such far-flung places as Washington State, Michigan, Texas, and New Mexico. The aforementioned prohibition by the Santa Ana division of the California Water Quality Board was triggered by the dairies' contamination of groundwater, the drinking water supply for a massive urban population.

The state and federal agencies charged with protecting the environment and human health found themselves the targets of political pressure brought about by state legislators under the sway of the dairy industry. The ISDA, for example, would have just ignored the complaints regarding the treatment of cows at Tuls's dairy operation were it not for local activists taking these problems to the media. Any attempt to regulate the large dairies unleashed political reactions. Any attempts to enforce air-emission or water-discharge permits were resisted vehemently by the dairies and elected representatives. There have been successful citizens' suits, brought under the federal Clean Air Act and Clean Water Act, but these have only forced the defendants' operations to comply with weak air and water laws and regulations and had little or no effect on the industry as a whole.

## Inside the Machine

Ignoring the sign reading: ALL VISITORS MUST SIGN-IN AT THE OFFICE, we proceeded up the wooden stairs to the "observation area." I was informed that if the owner knew that we were here, we would be either denied access, closely supervised, or arrested for trespassing. The observation area was located about twenty-five feet above the milking carousel. Flies covered the glassed-in area. We were in a large metal building; behind us were the enormous tanks that contained and chilled the milk. Lined up outside the building were gleaming tanker trucks, with hoses attached like piglets at a sow's teats. A bank of computers ran along the opposite wall. Among other, more mundane, functions, these computers, we learned later from a friendly employee, were used to keep track of each cow's production.

But it was what we found below that commanded our attention. The milking carousel accommodates about one hundred cows, and it turns slowly. A couple of workers ensure that the cows are lined up properly to get on the wheel. As a cow enters the empty stanchion, vacated by the previous cow who has been gently bumped in the head by a tire affixed above the wheel, two employees begin cleansing the udder. Two other workers attach the milking suction cups, which are in turn affixed to pipes that transport the milk to the holding and cooling tanks.

Every half hour or so, a flush system spreads water across the floor. This water carries the cow pies and copious volumes of urine down grated drains and through pipes to the cesspit outside. From there, fixed irrigation lines transport the liquefied wastes to center-pivot sprayers. The sprayers, moving in huge slow circles, apply the wastes to the fields adjacent to the milking and feeding center. Each cow has a computer chip implanted in her ear. A tracking device mounted on the stanchion relays production information to the central data bank, stored on one of the computers in the observation area. If the cow falls below a certain expected quota (the national average is about 260 pounds of milk per week), she is "culled" from the milking herd, sent to a slaughterhouse, and converted into ground beef. In 2002, over 65 percent of Idaho's slaughterhouse beef was from culled dairy cows. Each cow is provided ground feeds, a "proprietary" mixture likely consisting of grains, antibiotics, appetite enhancers, and other additives, and as the carousel slowly makes its way around, and if all goes as preprogrammed, the cow will finish the feeds and be milked-out by the time the tire bumps her head, causing her to back off the carousel to make room for the next cow.

And so it went. Cow after cow, around and around, twenty-four hours a day, seven days a week. Each cow in this herd of 5,000 or so was milked at least twice a day. (Efforts have been made to boost the schedule to three times per day, but the results have been inconclusive. There is some evidence that milking more than twice per day actually results in lowered production—and higher labor costs.)

After observing one complete rotation of this Road Warrior–like mechanization, part *Star Wars,* part Rube Goldberg, we discussed the computer operations with an employee. This employee apparently did not view us as representing any sort of threat, but after our discussion we slipped quietly back down the wooden stairs. We drove away, in complete silence, past row after row of cows under metal roofs on concrete floors. They were lined up at feeding troughs from which they took in the compounds that would make them eat more feeds, drink lots of water, and give more milk.

## Not Milk

There are those who claim, based upon much documentation, that milk, as currently produced, presents a clear and present danger to human health. These claims are summarized in a 1997 book, by neuroscientist Robert Cohen, titled *Milk, the Deadly Poison* and elaborated upon on practically a daily basis on a Web site (www.notmilk.com). One of the principal targets is rBGH. Bovine Growth Hormone (BGH) is a "natural" compound found in all dairy cows, but the genetically altered version of this hormone has aroused the ire of activists and more traditional dairy farmers. The *r* indicates that BGH has been altered—and is short for *recombinant,* meaning the compound has been combined with genes from other organisms. In the case of rBGH, the combination is, unbelievably, with *E. coli.*

The FDA, under pressure from Monsanto, which is the developer and the patent holder of rBGH, and in response to a scientific report compiled by scientists under contract with Monsanto, declared in 1993 that milk produced with rBGH was essentially "biologically indistinguishable" from milk with natural BGH. The FDA ordered that milk produced without rBGH could not be so labeled, and Monsanto has filed lawsuits against dairies and dairy co-ops that have placed a notice on their milk products that these were produced "rBGH-free."

There is little doubt that the injection of rBGH increases

the milk production of a dairy cow. There is also little doubt that rBGH increases the likelihood of mastitis (an infection of the udders and teats of the cow) and shortens the productive life of the cow. Given there is a surplus of milk in this country, the only advantage of a cow producing even more milk is that the owner of the dairy gets rewarded with greater subsidies, and there is always a slaughterhouse market for culled cows. The use of rBGH is detrimental to cows in large dairies but quite beneficial to their owners.

The key word in the preceding sentence is *large*: Small, traditional dairies don't use rBGH; the costs are too high and the results mixed. These family-owned dairies typically don't view individual cows as mere milk machines requiring artificial means to produce as much milk as possible. Mastitis is an ailment to be treated—not a reason to send the infected cow to the slaughterhouse. Finally, traditional dairies tend to be more concerned about the lifetime production of a cow, not short-term production. In most areas, obtaining milk from dairies that don't use rBGH is easy. Even though, as mentioned earlier, the FDA prohibits such proclamations on milk cartons and other dairy product containers, it is relatively easy for a consumer to determine whether or not a product contains rBGH. Just contact the dairy and ask. If they won't tell you, it is safe to assume that they use it.

Is rBGH dangerous to human health? Did the report by Monsanto scientists force the FDA to make a decision detrimental to human health? The answers to these questions are not at all clear. Some evidence suggests that drinking large amounts of milk containing rBGH causes unusual weight gain. There is also some evidence indicating that rBGH causes the body to produce excessive amounts of IGF-I, an insulin critical in properly processing sugars, and hence leads to a greater incidence of diabetes. What Monsanto scientists missed, critics claim, was the unintended consequences of injections of rBGH into otherwise healthy cows.

European countries employ what is called the Precautionary Principle: When an activity threatens human health or the environment, precautionary measures are taken even if cause and effect relationships have not been fully established. This principle is applied when assessing whether or not a newly created compound should be used. As much attention is paid to determining the unintended consequences as is paid to developing the compound. Unfortunately, in this country the Precautionary Principle has been turned on its head: A compound is to be used and released unless and until harmful effects have been conclusively demonstrated. Under this standard, Monsanto can continue to market rBGH and large dairies may continue to use it unless and until studies demonstrate and prove beyond doubt that it is harmful to human health. Monsanto is not about to perform such studies. Neither is the National Institute of Health nor any other public or private funding entity. And since there is no proof rBGH presents a health threat, the CDC will collect no data. There is not now, and likely will not be, serious scientific inquiry into the harmful impacts, or unintended consequences, of rBGH. Therefore, use of this genetically modified compound will continue.

In addition to rBGH, large dairies also use antibiotics to increase production, even though a number of peer-reviewed scientific studies have revealed that antibiotics have no effect on milk production. While critical for treating certain specific human diseases, antibiotics do nothing to prevent or control the spread of such diseases. Indeed, as I will be discussing in much more detail later in this book, overuse of antibiotics in livestock operations, including dairies, decreases the effectiveness of these drugs in combating the very food-borne diseases contracted from meats and animal products.

Meanwhile, Robert Cohen labors on. In a reversal of the claims made for Victorian-era snake-oil formulas that were asserted to cure all ills, Cohen's NotMilk site claims that milk is an ill that resists all cures. No doubt some of what he says is true; pasteurization does, in fact, destroy vitamins and minerals. And there is little doubt that the Dairy Association with its "Got Milk" campaign exaggerates the beneficial aspects of this viscous white fluid. It should come as no surprise that Big Milk, the dairy industry, with access to the media, benefactors in the USDA, influence over legislators, and access to millions of dollars in advertising, is winning the battle for the hearts and minds of consumers.

## Veal—Don't Eat It

While there are a lot of questions about the healthfulness of milk and the continuing controversies about hormones and antibiotics, there is one thing the dairy industry does that is beyond all doubt truly reprehensible—and that I addressed briefly in the introduction. Female calves have the potential to develop into productive dairy cows, and there is a subsidiary "replacement" industry revolving around raising female calves, heifers, to replace culled dairy cows. No such market exists for male calves. Semen to impregnate cows to produce the replacements comes from a very few bulls selected as sperm donors because of their genetic makeup, which, it is hoped, will be passed on to their heirs. With artificial insemination the standard industry practice, impregnating an entire herd of cows requires a small amount of semen from an equally small number of bulls, and hence no demand for bull calves.

The market for dairy steers is also very limited. Angus and Hereford steers reach market weight much more rapidly than do dairy steers, and these breeds, or some cross such as "black white-face," animals with attributes of both their Angus and Hereford parents, are the predominant inhabitants of feed-lots. As a result, there is very little to be gained by raising a male dairy calf. It is simpler to just kill male baby calves shortly after birth. Those who escape this immediate fate are doomed to become veal. The life of a male calf raised for veal is hardly a life at all. Veal has high value because it is tender and pale and lacks the chewiness of steak. This tenderness is due to a lack of muscles. The calf is contained in a tiny stall in which any movement is all but impossible. The animal is tethered and receives neither protein nor even iron in his feed. At the slaughterhouse, the calf is bled out, so that no taint of red enters the meat.

This, then, is how veal gets produced: A calf is taken from his mother, placed in a small pen, tethered so that movement is impossible, then fed a bland no-protein diet. He becomes anemic and diseased. Then he is drained of his blood and killed.

Thankfully, because public awareness of this horror has led to a decline in demand and consequent reduction in price per pound, currently around $85 per hundredweight or 85 cents per pound, and increased costs in producing veal, fewer male calves suffer this horrible fate. While I have not in this book advocated or promoted a vegetarian or vegan lifestyle but rather suggest that it is preferable to buy meats, milk, and eggs from local, diversified farms that treat food animals with respect and good husbandry, there is, however, simply no way to produce veal without torture. If this book convinces you of nothing else, let it convince you of this:

Don't buy veal. Don't eat veal. Don't patronize any restaurant that has veal on its menu—and be sure to tell them why you are not eating there.

# BIG BEEF

## The Slaughterhouse Rules

A COUPLE OF YEARS AGO, ALONG WITH THREE ANTI–
Big Milk activists, I flew over the Snake River in Idaho. We
spotted more dairies than we could count, as well as one gigantic "shitfall" over the Snake River Canyon rim from a dairy
lagoon. We also saw the giant beef feedlot owned by J. R. Simplot of potato fame. It turns out that J. R. has invested in both
meat and potatoes. Within the canyon, in an area that we estimated to be at least half a mile wide, were housed, according
to people from the area we talked to, over 100,000 cattle. The
massive feedlot was located well above the highest flood level
and partially hidden by a rolling cloud of dust. That dust was
apparently composed of dried manure, because we could
smell dung in the airplane—and a quick glance at the altime-
ter revealed that we were flying over 4,000 feet above the river.

Yet even at this height, it was impossible to get the entire feed-lot into one camera view frame; it took three shots to capture the entire feedlot. One of my companions had a video camera, and she had to scan the feedlot while our small plane circled over it.

The Simplot feedlot likely bothered no one, in terms of either smell or flies. It was miles from the nearest dwelling. However, that it was located adjacent to the Snake River made it inevitable that there would be manure running off into this already damaged body of water. The Snake River is listed as "impaired" by the EPA.

Simplot is not atypical. Although these operations may contain hundreds of thousands of heads of steer, beef feedlots have not yet attracted the ire of local residents nearly as much as those operations involving hogs, dairy, chickens, or salmon. There are likely several reasons for this. The first is that feed-lots have thus far been located in sparsely populated areas, such as those in western states. Second, there isn't much rainfall in these areas, and consequently there is not much pollution of surface waters. Third, feedlots don't use a wet-handling system, as can be attested to by anyone who has traveled through western states and seen steers standing atop huge piles of dried manure. Flies and odor are therefore not as prevalent. Fourth, beef feces do not have nearly the stink quotient as does a similar amount of crap from other farm animals. It's not that beef shit doesn't smell, just that it doesn't smell as bad. Fifth, the feedlots have been located in the same areas for years. Anyone who objected to the smells and sounds either moved out long before or adjusted. (One exception to this is Greeley, Colorado, where the town built up around the huge feedlots.) Sixth, most of the residents near feedlots have professional connections to them. The residents either work at the feedlot or adjacent slaughterhouse or are in a business (realty, insurance, banking) that depends on the feedlot's existence.

These are the reasons beef feedlots have not been perceived of as affecting the quality of life in the areas where they are located. Of course there are concerns related to the animals' welfare, but these appear to be less severe in the feedlot operations. While the cattle are confined in a small area without shade or any protection from wind, rain, or snow, they are not kept indoors and in general are provided with sufficient room to move around, as well as plenty of access to feed and water. Nonetheless, anyone who has visited these massive operations is haunted by the sight of steers standing atop those piles of manure, looking off to the far horizon, lowing to be free. Of course, that is an anthropomorphic view, to be sure. Yet when contrasted to the sight of contented cattle grazing in a pasture, the feedlot scenario worsens.

While some feedlot owners own all of the cattle contained therein, others have contracted with individual ranchers to "finish out" the steers—in more local terms, this gets translated as "gettin' 'em fattened up for market." The steers probably started out on pasture, grazing on grasses. Then, to maximize weight and profit by producing beef that is marbled with fat, the rancher contracts with a feedlot to take on the steers during the last six months or so. Grain-fed beef steers tend to develop more fat in their muscles, which in turn makes the beef taste "beefier." Grass-fed beef steers don't develop this fat; cattle that remain on pasture until slaughtered have greatly reduced levels of fat—so much so that eating this meat will actually result in lowered cholesterol levels in the consumer. Moreover, due to the decreased levels of fat, grass-fed beef contains fewer calories.

Feedlots use their own special formulas, which they generally do not divulge; in fact, the USDA and state agricultural departments deem these feed contents "proprietary." The feeds are mostly composed of corn—which in itself has been a bit controversial among those who monitor its healthiness. But it is more than likely that most of the feeds contain growth hormones and appetite enhancers, as well as antibiotics, since cattle's digestive systems are not "equipped" to handle grains. Here are a few of the other possible ingredients as analyzed from acquired samples. All or just some of these may be present: chlortetracycline, bacitracin, methylene disalicylate, erythromycin, tylosin oxytetracycline, sulfamethazine, ethlenediamine dihydroiodide, lasacloid sodium, monensin, melengestrol acetate, zeronal, testosterone, estradiol benzoate, sodium bicarbonate, poloxaline, propionic acid, chicken manure, cattle manure, chocolate, stale pastries, cement dust, molasses, candy, urea, hooves, feathers, meat scraps (but not from ruminants, as that has now been banned due to BSE), fish meal, pasta, peanut skins, brewery wastes, cardboard, corn silage, Genetically Modified Organisms (GMO) grains, and various pesticides.

These are the additives that have caused the most concern among health professionals. As has been seen in other farm animals, daily subtherapeutic doses of antibiotics result in the production of pathogens resistant to the very antibiotics used to treat diseases resulting from these organisms. Growth hormones, including steroids, are not passed through the steers' digestive tracts but stay in the meats we eat.

## The Slaughterhouse Floor

Thus far I have not focused much on the slaughterhouses, except to note that the speed of their operations has increased to the point that it has become nearly inevitable that contaminated meats will reach the consumers. One common component of the meat industry—whether we are discussing chickens, steers, hogs, or salmon—is the increasing likelihood of the animals' ingesting material that is not meat; this includes feces, dirt, slaughterhouse debris, feathers, scales, pus, and other unsavory items. These items, however distasteful, won't kill you when you ingest them through meat. What will kill you—at least make you very sick—is the pathogens contained in meat products as well as milk and eggs. The most deadly is a form found in the guts of animals tagged *Escheria coli* 0157:H7. *E. coli* was not even identified until 1982; it had simply not been a problem when meats came from smaller slaughterhouses and packing plants.

The CDC report 73,000 cases of *E. coli* infection and sixty-one deaths in the United States every year. The symptoms include bloody diarrhea and even kidney failure. The chief cause is ground beef that is contaminated, though infection can sometimes happen from person-to-person contact, ingestion of raw milk, or swimming in water that has been contaminated with sewage. The CDC recommend cooking ground beef, drinking only pasteurized milk, and washing hands carefully.

There are other forms of pathogens behind food-borne illnesses: Camphylobacter, salmonella, and listeria are some of
the most common. Salmonella probably causes the most distress, but except among the very young, the very old, and other
at-risk populations, it is seldom fatal, and it may cause nothing
more than diarrhea and vomiting. These symptoms occur anywhere between several hours and several days after ingestion
of contaminated foods. That is why it is sometimes hard to
make a connection between the outbreak and a particular
food. Moreover, the symptoms can sometimes be as mild as a
mere stomach upset, and doctors attribute them to the flu.
The CDC concede that the number of salmonella cases reported each year represents only the tip of the iceberg and report that there are 40,000 reported outbreaks of salmonella
annually, but that the "actual number of infections may be
thirty or more times greater."

There is no doubt among CDC scientists that contamination of meats—particularly ground meats, such as hamburger—is the result of slaughter and grinding. Yet the Food
Safety and Inspection Service of the USDA (USDA/FSIS) has
no system in place to alert consumers to potential contamination. The USDA/FSIS meat inspectors—whose numbers have
lately been greatly reduced—are trained to detect sick cows
and identify problems in the animals' intestines and body organs and the meat products. Yet none of their efforts are
geared toward identifying the pathogens responsible for these
symptoms. The technology is readily available; it is simply not
used by meat inspectors. In effect, meat inspectors use consumers to identify an outbreak. When we become ill after a
visit to a fast-food restaurant or a school cafeteria or after eat-

ing meats that have been purchased at the supermarket, then and only then does a recall of contaminated meats occur. By then, it is of course too late, as was the case with the massive recall of ground beef from the Greeley, Colorado, packing plant owned by ConAgra on June 30, 2002; by the time it had taken place, most of the meat had been consumed and consumers were already severely ill. Children had either died or suffered illnesses that would keep them from leading normal lives.

The recall, which involved 18.6 million pounds of meat, took place after nineteen people in a number of states became ill after eating meat packaged at the ConAgra plant. The federal government wasn't notified until July 19, when it immediately sent teams out to Greeley. Some within the meat industry complained that the scope of the recall was uncalled-for. As reported in the *New York Times* on July 20, Rosemary Mucklow, executive of the National Meat Association, said, "We always want to protect the public's health, but I think this recall is excessive. We know the meat produced on May 31 has caused illness. So to recall a large quantity of untested meat, especially meat that has been in circulation for three months, may be an effort that is not justified." The *Times* also quoted Steven Cohen, a spokesman for the USDA/FSIS, as saying that it had been necessary for the recall to cover three months of production because *E. coli* had been sporadically detected even before the outbreak of illness. "To be absolutely sure, it is better to err on the side of caution," said Cohen. The *Times* also quoted labor officials who had been complaining for quite some time that ConAgra's employees, who were not unionized, were insufficiently trained. Many were immigrants and could not read or write English and thus were unable to follow the packaging procedures.

In recent years, there have been many instances of beef products being recalled because of bacteria. In 2003, the CDC reported that there were seven major USDA/FSIS recalls of contaminated beef products. These were mostly attributable to E. coli but also included ground beef laced with pieces of glass as well as the infamous "downer cow" meats from the state of Washington.

As slaughterhouses crank up line speeds to disassemble more animals per day, their reliance on this pool of workers to meet new quotas grows. Coupled with the USDA/FSIS's turning over of much of the oversight for proper sanitation procedures to the slaughterhouses themselves, the fox, once again, is guarding the henhouse.

"You start out on the kill floor, it kind of gets to you. All those living animals, stunned, stuck, and skinned," explained "Bill Buck," a slaughterhouse worker. "Then after a few days and they just keep coming, you get to where they aren't even living things anymore. They're just things. One after another. They keep coming and coming and coming. On my line, we kill four hundred an hour. If any of them puts up any kind of resistance, this is just viewed as a frustration. Some of the guys take it out on the animals. They hit 'em with crowbars even though these aren't even supposed to be in the plant, they stick the stun gun in their eyes, or they don't even bother stunning them, just hang 'em on the chain squirming and struggling.

"After a while, you don't even think about it. You just do what you're supposed to do. But it gets to you in ways that you don't even know about or think about. Almost everybody on the kill floor goes down to the bar after the shift. Some of them don't go home until they're so drunk they can hardly stand up. Then they beat up their wife or their kids.

"They go home and treat their family like they're on the kill floor. Or they get in fights. They go to jail. After you've worked on the kill floor covered in blood and gore, it's like being in combat. It gets to you." Bill Buck stared into his empty beer bottle as if it contained answers.

What happens in a slaughterhouse is never pretty: There is no way to make killing animals pleasant either for the animals or for those who kill them. However, some ways are more humane than others. And there are without question ways to ensure that the meat products that come out of the slaughterhouses and packing plants are safe enough to eat. It is not a coincidence that more humane slaughter practices result in safer meat products. It used to be that the slaughterhouse workers' jobs were completed at the "sawing in half" part—then the sides of beef were delivered in refrigerated trucks to butcher shops and supermarkets for further processing. However, there are very few butcher shops still operating in the United States and supermarkets want the meats to arrive precut and prepackaged. So the slaughterhouse has evolved into a disassembly plant, slicing animals into the retail portions and packaging these for shipping and delivery.

Since 1958, when then-senator from Minnesota Hubert Humphrey introduced the Humane Slaughter Act, which passed and subsequently became law, USC Title 7, Chapter 48, slaughterhouses have been held to the following standard:

### Sec. 1902.—Humane Methods

No method of slaughtering or handling in connection with slaughtering shall be deemed to comply with the public policy of the United States unless it is humane. Either of the following two methods of slaughtering and handling are hereby found to be humane:

(a) in the case of cattle, calves, horses, mules, sheep, swine, and other livestock, all animals are rendered insensible to pain by a single blow or gunshot or an electrical, chemical or other means that is rapid and effective, before being shackled, hoisted, thrown, cast, or cut.

Subsection (b) of the preceding law involves "ritual slaughtering" by religious groups and is essentially an exemption to subsection (a).

Slaughterhouses use a stun gun to "render" an animal "insensible." These guns deliver either a bolt driven by compressed air or an electroshock. In the beef-packing industry, bolts are normally used (some form of electrical stunning or paralysis is used for broilers and hogs). The slaughtering process, if followed correctly, is designed for efficient killing and disassembly of a steer, bull, or cow:

1. The animal is herded into a stanchion and its head is locked in place.

2. The "knocker" places the stun gun in the middle of the animal's forehead and depresses the trigger. The bolt slams into and through the animal's skull.

3. The "catcher" attaches a shackle to one of the rear legs of the animal and it is hoisted onto the "chain"—the conveyor that will transport the carcass through the disassembly process.

4. At this point, the animal is alive, although stunned into insensibility. The "sticker" slices through the carotid artery and the animal bleeds out and dies.

5. The skinners remove the hide, beginning at the head.

6. The head and intestines are removed.

7. The animal is cut in two, so that each part becomes a "side of beef." Since only one hind leg has been shackled to the chain, at this point a shackle is attached to the hind leg of the unattached half.

8. The two halves are cut into the various components for packaging and shipping. Parts that are unusable and entire carcasses of bulls, dairy culls, and other undesirable animals are ground up in an enormous grinding machine.

That is how it is supposed to be. Often what happens is that for a variety of reasons, some related earlier by the slaughterhouse worker, the animal is not properly stunned and arrives at the station of the sticker alive and kicking. The sticker will then attempt to cut the poor animal's carotid artery but has to defend himself against being kicked, butted, or bitten. This often prevents successful severing of the artery and the shackled steer literally gets skinned alive. More out of self-interest than humaneness, the skinners kill the animal by means of a heavy blunt instrument. By this time, the animal's hide has become covered with dung, some of which gets transferred to the meat. A frightened animal—one that is being slammed with a bolt, hung on a shackle, stabbed, and beaten—will likely lose control of its sphincter muscles and quite literally shit all over, emptying the contents of the digestive tract onto the hide and the meat.

Most slaughterhouses use several different methods to try to remove feces and associated contaminants, such as *E. coli* and other pathogens, from the meats—as they make their way down the line, the carcass and its components may be exposed to water sprays, steaming, and steam vacuuming. None of these methods are entirely effective at removing all microscopic pathogens, which are most likely to turn up in ground meats. The grinding process exposes large surface areas to such contaminants; each particle becomes a potential carrier. Unbelievably, the ground meats, which will be made into hamburgers in your kitchen or in fast-food restaurants, are not examined for bacteria before packaging. In addition to ground beef, those carefully wrapped cellophane and Styrofoam packages may contain deadly germs.

No USDA/FSIS inspector will be present during this whole messy and sometimes horrific process. The inspectors may have been in the yard and set aside any animals that showed signs of disability or any cows that were "3-D" (dead, down, or diseased). The inspectors may have also been inside the plant, looking for the physical manifestations of disease—ulcers, sores, and other obvious discolorations in the meats—or examining the internal organs that were removed in the gutting process to see if they show any signs of disease. But they won't be there to see what happens to either the animal or the meat during slaughtering.

The faster the line, the more likely that animals will not be properly stunned, and therefore the higher the likelihood that they will void their bowels and soil their hides. The lines run so fast that the slaughterhouse workers cannot keep up; the typical beef slaughterhouse kills 6,400 animals per day in only two shifts. While workers and USDA/FSIS inspectors have the authority to shut off the line in the event that something goes wrong, they almost never do. The worker would be fired, and the USDA inspector would be transferred. As one former inspector stated, "This is the only job where the government employee works at the pleasure of a private company."

The turnover rate in some slaughterhouses is 100 percent per year: Every employee hired leaves before completing a year of work. Little wonder why. Poor training makes this a very dangerous job. In most cases, it consists of handing these unskilled workers a sharp knife and telling them to "cut here." A "knocker" told me that his training was limited to a foreman showing him a photo of a cow's head with an "x" on it illustrating where he was to place the stun gun. Injuries are inevitable. Lacerations in slaughterhouses are common, but undocumented migrant workers are unlikely to complain to state or federal agencies. Repetitive motion injuries—cutting the same portion of meat hour after hour day after day—result in paralysis or excruciating pain. This high turnover rate actually benefits the company, since there is no need to provide insurance or sick leave.

## Have Another Cup of Coffee and Pray

Compounding the problem is the consolidation of the industry. The number of beef companies continues to shrink; most recently IBP, the biggest of the big, was purchased by Tyson. The companies that own the feedlots also own the slaughterhouses and processing plants. With the speed of the line, the unskilled nature of the workforce, and the inability of meat inspectors to do their job, what is surprising is that food-borne illnesses are not more common. Consumers have bought into the idea that it's their responsibility to ensure that meat is safe by cooking it thoroughly to kill the pathogens lurking inside. This is not a solution—even thorough cooking does not eliminate the possibility of contracting meat- and egg-borne pathogens. To guarantee our safety, a much more manageable system of slaughter, one where a few or a few hundred steers are processed each day and one where modern technologies could detect the presence of deadly pathogens *before* the meat leaves the plant, is necessary.

Also necessary is a change in the USDA/FSIS's relying on the meatpacking industry to regulate themselves instead of cracking down on the industry. According to the USDA/FSIS, companies need to be held more accountable for ensuring that their products are safe and healthy. That, in fact, should be the goal of the slaughterhouse industry. But this was compromised when the Clinton administration placed former executives of the slaughterhouse industry's lobbying organization, the American Meat Institute, in charge at the USDA and the USDA/FSIS. Upon taking office, Pres. George W. Bush appointed Anne Venneman, an executive with Monsanto, secretary of agriculture. With such former executives of industry in control, the USDA/FSIS promoted and eventually promulgated as a regulation a system called by the optimistic title Hazard Analysis and Critical Control Point (HACCP or phonetically "hassip"). With their hands effectively tied, federal meat inspectors claimed that *HACCP* stood for "Have Another Cup of Coffee and Pray."

In theory, the system was sound. The slaughterhouse would identify critical points in the slaughter/disassembly process where contamination was likely to occur and then design appropriate decontamination methods for those points. The USDA/FSIS would review the plans and either approve or disapprove of the methods. Once methods were approved, meat inspectors would monitor the decontamination points to ensure that the company complied. There are several problems with this:

1. The company doesn't make money taking contaminated products off the line.

2. The USDA/FSIS promptly "retired" about fourteen hundred meat inspectors.

3. The meat inspectors in charge of checking HACCP mostly ended up reviewing paperwork.

4. As usual, a USDA/FSIS inspector who indicated disapproval of company plans risked harassment and disciplinary action.

5. There was no final check or decontamination of ground beef. Grinding, the final step in the disassembly process, is not identified as a point of contamination and is not subjected to any scrutiny.

Consequently, there have been several outbreaks of *E. coli* since the implementation of HACCP in 1999, with the seven major recalls in 2003 representing the tip of the iceberg. As has been discussed, meat inspectors are quite reluctant to stop the line and they have no legal ability to mandate recalls. There is absolutely no indication that this system is any better than what it replaced, and there is some evidence that it may actually be worse. There has been no decrease in the number of illnesses or deaths attributed to contaminated meats and certainly no decrease in the amounts of contaminated meats reaching the consumer. From the perspective of the meat-packing industry, HACCP is a striking success. For those eating their products, it is a dismal failure, and those who eat meat remain at risk.

It is a shame that it takes a near tragedy to call for any change in "business as usual" for the USDA and the meat industry. Were it not for a downer cow testing positive for BSE and the resultant public horror at discovering that their hamburger or steak may have come from an animal that was so sick it couldn't stand up, it is likely that the meat from downer cows would still be served at fast-food joints. However, the inspection system to prevent tainted meats from entering the market remains under the control of the industry that stands to profit. Until changes are made in this inspection system— including the employment of new technologies—we are the canaries in the coal mine for discovering the hazards of the meat we eat.

# BIG FISH

## Our Boats Are Rotting on the Beach

"WE GET ABOUT FIFTEEN TO TWENTY CENTS A POUND for quality salmon—sockeye, pinks—where in the past we got anywhere from three-fifty to four dollars a pound. The salmon farms have just glutted the market and driven the prices way down," relayed Brian Wadhams of the First Nation peoples of British Columbia.

"We don't hardly even try to catch fish anymore. Some of us do it, just because that's what we've always done and because we have boats and equipment to pay for. But we're able to fish such a short time, and then we don't get a living wage even for that short time. There's not even a market for our boats; they're just rotting on the shore."

The Georgia Strait is a large body of salt water, surrounded by heavily timbered mountains, between the mass of Vancouver Island and the mainland of British Columbia. While the strait occasionally gets rough, it is nothing like the open Pacific Ocean. For this reason, it has been fished by native peoples since time immemorial. In the 1950s, over 5,000 commercial salmon-fishing boats plied the glistening waters off the mostly protected coast of British Columbia. Now the strait is "home" to gigantic salmon pens, enclosures owned primarily by multinational corporations that raise millions of salmon per year. As the salmon pens moved in, the native fishing industry gradually declined until by the late 1980s the corporations had taken over and the once-swarming fishing fleet was all but gone.

"Then," stated Wadhams, "the British Columbian government came up with this idea that was supposed to restore our native fishery. They decided that the fleet should be cut in half. So, they reduced the number of boats that could be on the water, reduced the number of days and the licenses, put limits on the days and hours that we could fish . . . and it all went belly up. The ones who benefited were the ones with the most money. They bought up the licenses of the little guys, and took over the industry.

"As best we can tell, the whole thing has been mismanaged, but mismanaged in such a way that the large commercial companies and the salmon-pen corporations benefited. Lots of old-time fishermen went bankrupt. It's simply impossible to make a living fishing eighteen to thirty-six hours per year, with the price of salmon what it is.

"We were told that the Atlantic salmon in the pens would, one, never escape to compete with wild salmon, two, never intermingle with the wild salmon, three, never enter our rivers

and streams, and four, never spawn. All this was just flat un-
true and all of these things that we were told could 'never happen' are happening.

"Rather than protecting the wild salmon stocks and the environment, the Federal and Provincial Governments have devoted much time and attention to protecting an industry that
has decimated our wild stocks and has destroyed the environment—and the local economy.

"Now, villages up and down the coast have high unemployment and have the whole gamut of social ills, but there has
been little available in the way of assistance from the government. We are just left to deal with it."

The plan Wadhams describes was conceived in the mid-
1990s by then minister of fisheries and oceans Fred Mifflin
and was tagged the "Mifflin Plan." Its goal was simple: to cut
the fishing fleet in half, reduce the number of days that a boat
could fish, and therefore, it was assumed, cut the number of
fish caught by at least one-half. The results were exactly opposite. Licenses were bought up and "stacked" by the biggest
companies and multiple-boat owners while coastal communities got cut out. The only way to pay for the costs of the
stacked licenses was to catch more fish. The Mifflin Plan to reduce the catch of native salmon was turned on its head.

In the meantime, the salmon farms filled the market with
cheap fish and filled the Georgia Strait with pollution and escaped salmon. The result was complete destruction of what
little was left of the economy for small, independent boat
owners and coastal communities. The Mifflin Plan was an un-
mitigated disaster. Now there are almost no boats plying the

waters of the strait in search of salmon and the industry that once kept thousands of First Nation community members employed up and down the coast has pushed them out.

## Farming Fish

Today the menus of mid- and up-scale restaurants almost inevitably include "farm-raised" or "Atlantic" salmon. Baked, fried, broiled, or stuffed, it has become a standard offering, even from establishments that claim to be sensitive to how their meats are raised. In 2001, the last year for which numbers are available, commercially produced fish—the bulk of which are salmon—amounted to 214 million pounds.

In addition to the destruction of indigenous fishing industries, consider this:

- The Atlantic salmon on the menu does not come from anywhere near the Atlantic Ocean. It is a species of salmon that originally came from the Atlantic but is now primarily raised in gigantic fish pens in the Pacific Ocean. There are a few pens in the North Atlantic of Scotland and Norway.
- The wild North Atlantic salmon is an endangered species and afforded the protections of the Endangered Species Act. It may not be taken for any purpose, commercial or otherwise, and cannot be caught or served.
- The escape and survival of a few Atlantic salmon from the Pacific pens—if 40,000 a year can be considered "a few"—has led to crossbreeding and com-

petition for food with native Pacific coast salmon subspecies that may eventually lead to the demise of native stocks.

- Rearing Atlantic salmon in these enormous multi-tiered pens has created "dead zones" in the area of the ocean under and around the pens as feces, excess foods, and harmful feed additives stack up on the seafloor. Salmon pens have also led to an infestation of "sea lice," which prey on both introduced and native salmon stocks.

- Heavy metals and toxic compounds, including PCBs (polychlorinated biphenyls), are concentrated in the feeds provided to the penned salmon and remain in the fillet on your plate.

- To prevent the damage caused by pens, a federal judge in Portland, Maine, essentially banned salmon farming in Maine's offshore waters. The state of Alaska has also banned salmon pens from its waters, in order to protect native stocks and the Alaskan fishing industry.

This is in part the result of the multinational corporations' takeover of the industry. In the case of salmon farming, the industry is dominated by Norwegian and Dutch corporations.

Nutreco, an Amsterdam-based corporation, is the market leader, and it is a prime example of the global nature of the industry as a whole. It states in its financial reports that it is involved in two major enterprises: aquaculture and agriculture, and lists the following as principal companies held by Nutreco Holding NV in the area of aquaculture:

| | |
|---|---|
| Australia | Gibson's Ltd., Launceton, Tasmania |
| Canada | Marine Harvest Canada Farming, Kitchener |
| | Nutreco Canada, Inc., Toronto |
| Chile | Marine Harvest S.A., Puerto Monte (*sic*) |
| | Nutreco Chile Ltd., Santiago |
| France | Marine Harvest Valmer S.A., Chateaugiron |
| | Trouw France S.A., Vervins |
| Germany | Trouw Nutrition Deutschland GmbH |
| Ireland | Marine Harvest Fanad Ltd., Letterkenny |
| | Trouw Aquaculture Ltd., Roman Island |
| Japan | Nutreco Aquaculture Japan, Inc., Fukuoka |
| | Yamaha Nutreco Aquatech KK., Fukoka |
| | (50 percent holding) |
| Norway | Atlantic Halibut AS, Hjilmeland |
| | (62 percent holding) |
| | Cod Culture Norway AS, Oygarden |
| | (56.14 percent holding) |
| | Marine Harvest AS, Bergen |
| | Marine Harvest Norway, Bergen |
| | Marine Harvest Rogaland AS, Hjelmeland |
| | (62 percent holding) |
| | Mowi AS, Bergen |
| | Nutreco Aquaculture Research Centre AS, Stavanger |
| | Skretting AS, Stavanger |
| Spain | Trouw Espana S.A., Burgos |
| Turkey | Trouw Yem Ticaret Anonim Sirketi, Bodrum |
| | (99 percent holding) |
| United Kingdom | Marine Harvest Scotland Ltd., Edinburgh |
| | Trouw (UK) Ltd., Wincham |

In Nutreco's other major enterprise, agriculture, it holds outright or has a majority interest in companies in the Netherlands (15), Belgium (5), Brazil, Canada (2), China, Cyprus, Denmark, France, and Germany (4 each), Greece and Hungary (2 each), Italy (4), Mexico, Poland, and Portugal (2 each), Romania and Spain (12 each), the United Kingdom (3), and the United States of America (2). These extensive holdings are kept low-profile. Except for Marine Harvest, its holdings are essentially enterprises unknown to the consuming public. While the list of countries and companies is telling enough, the extent of Nutreco's reach is even worse when examined more closely. In Chile, for example, where Nutreco owns just two companies engaged in aquaculture, it has thirty salmon farms in this country or in its coastal waters. The net sales in 2002 from all operations was EUR$3,810,000,000.00, with aquaculture operations accounting for EUR$507,000,000. (While there are variations in the value of currencies, and subsequent fluctuations in the monetary exchange rate, at present a "Euro dollar" is worth about 1.25 U.S. dollars.) And this is just one company. There are at least ten doing business in the waters of British Columbia's Georgia Strait (see appendix A). These companies have been busily buying out owners of individual salmon pen clusters with the same detrimental results as has been seen in the other food-production sectors. Large corporations' operations are dominated by profits.

Most concerns and controversy surround "fish farming" in salt waters, like that of the penned Atlantic salmon. As best as can be determined, the problems cited earlier and detailed here do not apply to freshwater fish farms. Termed *aquaculture*, these operations are currently focused on catfish, with a newly emerging market for tilapia, a freshwater fish of the bass family, formerly of South and Central America. While there are some concerns about discharges from inland fish farms, specifically related to uneaten and dissolved feed pellets and fish feces, these facilities are required to obtain a permit from the state agency or U.S. EPA, with provisions that regulate what is discharged. While the permits are lightly enforced, these operations are required to submit Discharge Monitoring Reports to the state environmental agency and these reports are available for public viewing. However, since the salmon pens are located in seawater, mostly in bays and inlets protected from storms and heavy waves, there is no requirement for a state or federal wastewater discharge permit, nor is there any requirement that the feces, uneaten food, medicinals (mostly in the form of antibiotics), and other detritus be treated.

There are two stages of salmon farming. The first, the freshwater phase, which naturally or normally occurs in inland streams, begins with combining the milt (sperm) and roe (egg) extracted from adult salmon that have been selected for superior characteristics, primarily growth and "hardiness." This stage includes the hatching of the fertilized eggs and the raising of the young salmon. The young salmon are called alevins, then parr, and then smolts. During the egg or hatching period, the water temperature and filtration system are critical. The temperature of the water should be about forty to forty-five degrees Fahrenheit, and the eggs must be kept free of silt and sediment. These factors are also critical in hatching of salmon eggs in natural conditions.

In the second phase, once the salmon reach the smolt stage, or a length of about five inches, they are transferred to the salmon pens. (There have been attempts to raise salmon in land-based saltwater systems, but with little success and prohibitive costs.) The pens or cages are located above water that is at least 100 feet deep, a necessity since the pens are large. Each pen is approximately thirty meters wide by thirty meters long by twenty meters deep and contains up to 50,000 salmon.

The pens are often clustered in groups of eight, twelve, or twenty to facilitate feeding, cleaning, and other services. The pens themselves are large frames of PVC or steel pipes and extend for a few feet above the water to prevent escapes; the top may be covered with netting to prevent predation by seabirds. The bottom is covered with a heavier mesh to keep marine predators, such as great white sharks, killer whales, and seals, from the caged salmon. These bottoms often become encrusted with barnacles or other shellfish and can also become clogged with algae, necessitating temporary lifting of the pens via a large crane so that the shellfish and algae can be removed. The pens are anchored to the seafloor to both stabilize the depth of the pens and to keep them from drifting away.

The salmon rely on food pellets for their nutrients. These pellets constitute a concentrated diet, designed to promote maximum and efficient growth. The exact composition of the pellets at each operation is somewhat secret in nature and considered a "proprietary" trade secret. However, the Georgia Strait Alliance in a letter to the British Columbia minister of agriculture states that the pellets are typically composed of: "15% slaughterhouse wastes, 30% from grain crops, and

56% from rendered fish, including significant quantities of anchovy and jack mackerel from Peru and Chile." The pellets are "shot" into the pens through plastic tubes. Some companies claim to have underwater cameras that carefully monitor the feeding to ensure that most or all of the pellets are consumed, thereby minimizing loss of unconsumed pellets to the seafloor. However, most companies rely on the appetites of the penned salmon to cause them to efficiently ingest the pellets. It is to the companies' benefit to ensure such efficiency, since feed costs represent one-third of the costs of production. It is estimated that overall costs now average about two dollars per pound.

Inevitably, however, some pellets are uneaten and drift to the seabed, where they contaminate the area and create a dead zone where no living organism can survive. Fish pellets contain a high concentration of certain toxic substances found naturally—at low, nonharmful levels—in almost all living organisms. But when marine organisms (anchovies and other small "bait fish") are "rendered" and concentrated into feed pellets, the process also concentrates PCBs and dioxins. The result, according to the BBC in a report on January 3, 2001, is that the uneaten pellets fall into the sediments on the ocean floor at toxic levels.

The ocean floor isn't the only place these toxins settle. There has been considerable concern raised in England and Scotland, which along with Norway lead the planet in fish farming, that the pellets introduce cancer-causing toxic chemicals into the flesh of the fish itself. Salmon eat the pellets, the contaminants are stored in the fat and muscle of the fish, and then we eat the fish, contaminants and all. According to a study conducted by Michael Easton, a Vancouver geneticist, the farmed salmon he tested had far higher levels of most contaminants than wild fish. The farmed fish contained nearly ten times the toxic load of some types of PCBs as wild salmon. Easton estimated that based on World Health Organization standards for PCB exposure, Canadians should not eat more than one to three meals of farmed salmon a week.

After the salmon have been in the pens for about two years, they are harvested. If all goes well, the largest salmon will weigh about ten pounds and the smallest around five pounds. The industry average is slightly less than nine pounds. Salmon must be harvested prior to reaching sexual maturity, as the meat becomes unpalatable at that point. Before being filleted, the salmon are not fed for several days so that no material remains in the digestive tract, fat is reduced, and supposedly the meat becomes firmer. The pens are raised to concentrate the fish, which are then collected in large baskets or removed by large "fish pumps." The salmon are then "subdued," bled out, gutted, and packaged in iced containers for shipping to distribution centers.

## Everything They Promised Would Not Happen Has Happened

Even under the best circumstances, the process doesn't run this smoothly or neatly. Given the inherent difficulties of trying to corral any living creature, as well as an unpredictable ocean environment, there are substantial pitfalls. Among them, water temperatures that are either too high or too low can upset the hatcheries and storms can damage the pens. The industry anticipates a certain loss and estimates that only a relative percentage of the eggs will hatch, that only a certain percentage of the hatched eggs will result in alevins, that only a certain percentage of the alevins will make it to the smolt stage, and that some salmon will die in the pens while others will escape.

The latter problem presents the largest difficulty for the salmon industry and the largest worry for marine biologists and the traditional salmon-fishing industry. Initially it was believed that the escaped Atlantic salmon were strangers in a strange land that would not survive and certainly would not crossbreed with native stocks. Those beliefs have proven to be false: Not only do some escaped salmon survive and compete with wild stocks for food in the open ocean, but also some have crossbred with native Pacific coast salmon. These native stocks, as we all know so well, return, with increasing difficulty, to the headwaters of the streams in which they were spawned. The crossbreeding of Atlantic and native salmon produces a fish that quite literally is confused—it does not know where it came from and spends its sexually active time roaming the open ocean. Fertility becomes nil in these fish, and an already-diminished supply of native salmon is further reduced. Eventually, it is feared, succeeding generations of native salmon will become even more infused with genetic imprinting from Atlantic salmon, until there are no runs up local streams.

These escapees also create another problem: They are voracious feeders and compete with the wild stocks for the smaller fish that make up the diet of wild salmon. While the industry claims that only a "few" salmon escape from the pens, these few add up to at least 40,000 Atlantic salmon escaping from the pens per year. These salmon have no tracking mechanisms to guide them to the streams of their birth since they were hatched in a tank, but some have been found in inland fresh-water streams, where they compete with the native stocks for a diminishing supply of foods and may even fertilize the eggs of native salmon.

A more immediate, and equally critical, problem is sea lice infestation. The sea louse is a type of small arthropodic para-site that may be found on both wild and farmed fish. *Lepeoph-theirus salmonis* and *Caligus clemensi* are the most common lice found in the Pacific. Sea lice affect salmon in a variety of ways: mainly by reducing fish growth; causing loss of scales, which leaves the fish open to secondary infections; and damag-ing fish flesh, which reduces marketability. While sea lice are a naturally occurring parasite of native or wild salmon, the con-centration of salmon in pens can lead to an epidemic of these parasites. Such an epidemic not only is very costly to the salmon farming industry but also can and has spread to native stocks.

Despite these threats to native stocks, the government of British Columbia, whose jurisdiction includes the Georgia Strait, seems to be more concerned with maintaining a healthy commercial fishing industry than protecting the indigenous fish and "salmon tribes." Even though outbreaks of sea lice have apparently been exacerbated by the salmon pens, the government chooses to concern itself with the transference of sea lice from wild salmon to farmed salmon. In February 2000, the British Columbian government established a sea lice mon-itoring program whose objective is to gather information on the levels of sea lice on farms and work with the industry to minimize the levels 'of lice. The government is also complicit with the fishing industry over the use of antibiotics in the salmon pens. As in other meat industries, antibiotics, such as tetracyclines and sulfas, are used to prevent and treat disease and, as well, to promote growth. Although there is cause to believe that the overuse of antibiotics in agriculture has negative effects, the Ministry of Agriculture, Food and Fisheries stated that "therapeutic use in aquaculture is used only to treat disease, judicious use of antibiotics in the aquaculture industry has been the norm and reducing antibiotic use remains a goal of all aquaculture producers."

Just as the U.S. government protects the interests of the swine, poultry, beef, and dairy industries, the British Columbian government acts as an advocate and a research arm for the salmon-pen industry. This choice is, of course, an economic one—if these decisions were based upon peer-reviewed scientific reports this government, and the governments of the other chief salmon-pen nations of Norway, Scotland, and Chile, would have banned the salmon farming industry and supported more traditional means of providing salmon fillets, such as has occurred in Alaska. But this provincial government has typically viewed its bountiful natural resources as "open for business" and has generally allowed various industries to operate at will, extracting private profits from public resources. Only after years of protests and a loud public outcry did British Columbia impose any limits on logging the Pacific Coast rain forests, even though the lands in question were in public ownership. A similar outcry is necessary to protect the waters. Until recently, opposition had not been well organized and certainly did not have sufficient funding to influence governmental decisions. As it stands now, according to critics, the British Columbian Ministry of Agriculture, Food and Fisheries acts as a lapdog for the salmon farming industry while ignoring the well-being of native peoples and citizens. But with the recent formation of organizations representing native fishing tribes and the entry of consumer groups into this fray, the government ministry is beginning to recognize that its actions have caused "unintended harm."

However, the multinational corporations that own the salmon industry have ensured that they will receive the support of governments in those coastal areas most conducive to plying their trade. In the United States, their influence is limited. Only areas along the coasts of Alaska, Maine, and Washington are conducive to salmon pens. Consequently, the multinationals have no reason to aggressively lobby U.S. governmental agencies and, not coincidentally, salmon farming has been banned or severely restricted. Salmon pens are banned in Alaska, in Maine a federal court ordered that no restocking occur, and Washington State has placed very stringent restrictions upon the industry.

The industrial production of salmon has much more to do with profit motives and controlling the market than it has to do with "feeding a hungry world." The only things being fed are the salmon and the corporate coffers. Meanwhile, local fishermen starve, the environment is polluted, and the fish are filled with toxins.

# CONCLUSION: STAY SMALL AND STAY ALIVE

### "Eating Is an Agricultural Act"

WHAT CAN WE DO IN THE FACE OF BIG AGRICULTURE? Wendell Berry said it best: "Eating is an agricultural act." What we put on our plates and into our mouths determines what is placed on restaurant menus and supermarket shelves. After learning how farm animals are raised and slaughtered, some people may choose to become vegan and eliminate meat and all animal products from their diet and their lifestyle. This is one option but, in my view, not the only one and certainly not the one that supports those who are engaged in sustainable agriculture. The most important thing you can do is simply take an interest in what you're eating. Ask questions: Who raised it and under what conditions? Above all, don't support corporate farms and their industrial methods—purchase meats, milk, and eggs that are produced on sustainable farms.

There are those who assert that there is no way to continue eating meat, milk, and eggs without being part of an inhumane and unhealthy system. They state that slaughterhouses are inherently cruel and morally wrong, that the practices of dairy farmers are abusive to cows, and that eggs cannot be produced without harming chickens. There is certainly some truth in this regarding slaughterhouses. There is no pleasant or wholesome way to kill an animal and cut it into palatable parts. But there are ways to make this process less objectionable—and those are required by law. The law is simply not being enforced. When it comes to milk and eggs, the cruelty aspect simply disappears. It is not only possible to obtain milk from cows and eggs from hens in a humane manner, but indeed, the cows and hens will be more productive from our perspective over a longer period if treated with respect.

To the astonishment of supermarket purchasing agents, consumers are demanding such products. The free-range, humanely treated, and organically grown foods are the fastest-growing agricultural sector. Supermarkets are all about making money, and if money can be made from selling free-range products or organic products or locally grown products, then that is what they will offer. Don't patronize a nearby supermarket until it starts offering products from sustainable growers—and let the supermarket know your reason for not buying its products. Ask supermarket managers the tough questions:

"Where do you buy your pork, your beef, your chicken? Are your salmon raised in pens?"

"Did you know that hormones, antibiotics, and appetite

enhancers were used in growing these fish, hogs, cows, or chickens?"

"Why didn't you buy from local growers, who don't use this stuff? Why don't you stock wild salmon?"

Use the power of the pocketbook to convince supermarkets that agribusiness meats are unacceptable and will rot in the case. Until that happens, appendix B will provide a starting point for locating sustainable producers in your area.

## Sustainable Farming

The way that meat, milk, and eggs are mass-produced by corporate agribusiness is the antithesis of sustainability. A sustainable farming system is one that essentially describes a circle. In this circle, each component depends upon all other components. The cow-and-calf operation produces manure, which nourishes the pasture, which produces the grasshoppers and plants upon which the chickens feed. Manure from the hog lot is used to fertilize the corn crop, part of which is fed back to the hogs. The surplus of both corn and hogs is sold to profit the farmer. Inputs, things that must be obtained from outside of the system, are minimal.

According to John Ikerd, a retired agricultural economist from the College of Agriculture at the University of Missouri, sustainability "is a long-run, people-centered concept. The purpose of sustainable development is to sustain a desirable quality of life for people, forever."

Professor Ikerd then discusses "sustainability" from an economics perspective: "An economics of sustainability must integrate the individual, social, and ecological economies. The purpose of sustainable economic policy must be to promote harmony and balance among the ecological, social, and individual economies. The three economies are inseparable dimensions of the same whole. We simply cannot do anything that affects one of the three economies without affecting the other two. If we are at a point of balance or harmony, we can't do anything to 'improve' one dimension without disturbing the balance, and thus making ourselves worse off overall than before. If we are out of balance, we can restore balance by devoting less time and energy to the dimension that we are 'overdoing,' and improve our overall well-being by actually doing less. An economics of sustainability will force us to rethink the conventional wisdom that more is better and to use our common sense to find success through harmony and balance."

Ikerd also states, "I didn't stop learning after I graduated from college." Clearly he understands that farming is in itself a manipulation of nature. Cultivation of grains and domestication of animals do not occur without disruptions of the natural process. But, as Ikerd relates, there are gradations of disruption, and he values that which disrupts least. Agribusiness corporations, with their focus on efficiency and monoculture, are acting at variance with all natural principles and hence are not "sustainable" over the long run. Those operations that embrace a whole farm system, where all is used and little is brought in, are most sustainable. Indeed, small, indigenous farms have been sustained for generations. These operations have minimal impacts on local ecosystems and are most supportive of local economies.

Organizations such as the National Campaign for Family

Farms and the Sustainable Agriculture Working Groups define a "sustainable and socially just" food system as a food system that would

- produce abundant, healthful food;
- provide just conditions and fair compensation for farmers and workers;
- strengthen local economies and communities;
- protect the natural resource base; and
- remain viable over the long term.

Sustainable agriculture presents solutions to almost all of the problems presented by corporate agribusiness:

- It is nonpolluting. There is no such thing as waste disposal, because waste does not need to be disposed of. It is used to produce crops that are fed back to the animals that produced the manure.
- It is not exploitative of workers. The employees on sustainable farms are paid a living wage, quite often receive a house and farm products, and become part of the family. Unfortunately, with the advent of the labor of migrant workers, "hired hands" are now viewed with disdain.
- It is more efficient.
- It is economically viable. Small, diversified independent farmers have successfully created their own markets, in most cases without any assistance from state or federal agricultural agencies. The quickly growing number of farmers' markets (see appendix

B) are proof that many consumers prefer products grown locally by independent farmers and growers.

- Products from sustainable producers are healthy and healthful. The products are generally free of pathogens and are laden with vitamins, minerals, and other healthy components. For at least four decades, *Organic Gardening and Farming*, a periodical published by Rodale Press, has conducted research that demonstrates the advantages of these products.

This isn't a wish list; those engaged in sustainable farming are already here.

Leron Small stood in the open door of his barn on his farm in central Pennsylvania looking up at the darkening sky and watching lightning bolts strike in his cornfield just on the other side of the road. Large raindrops began falling, each one raising a small cloud of dust and an equally small crater as the drops struck the ground.

The wind picked up and swept through the open barn door and out through the stalls in the "wintering shed" attached to the barn. Dust swirled through.

"Looks as if we're going to get some wind . . . but we can use the rain," Leron said, grinning, bristly graying hair sticking out from his "gimme" CAT cap. "That corn over there is starting to get a little dry. As long as the wind don't blow it down, the rain'll be good for it."

Inside the barn, Leron's milk cows were waiting placidly,

eating the grains and silage that Leron had put in the trough that ran the length of the milking parlor. Some of the younger cows were a bit nervous as the lightning bolts hurtled down and the thunder rumbled. These younger animals moved about restlessly while their heads were firmly locked into the stanchions. The older cows took it all in stride.

Leron hooked up the Surge milker to the suction pipe running along the top of the stanchions, ran the wide belt over the first cow, suspended the milking machine under the cow's stomach, washed the udder with a cleansing solution, and connected the "cups" to the cow's teats. The suction grasped the teats and the milker's pulsations began drawing the milk into the machine's five-gallon tank. Leron waited a few minutes, then crossed over to the other side and, repeating his motions, hooked the second milking machine to the cow waiting on that side. Neither cow had paid much attention to these intrusions but continued consuming the feeds.

"How many cows you got in here, Leron?"

"Right now, I'm milking thirty-six. But there's four more with their calves, and about ten more are dry. I've got fifty altogether, but I've never had all of them milking at the same time. Usually, I get about thirty-five to forty."

He went on, "The bulk tank holds three hundred gallons, and the Grade A truck comes by and pumps it out. Used to be, we had those damned ten-gallon milk cans—heavy sons-a-bitches, too. Where the bulk tank is now was sort of a walk-in cooler for those milk cans. The milk truck would come by and pick up the cans. It was a refrigerated box truck then, instead of today's tanker. I'd help the driver load them damned cans and he would leave the same number of empties. It's a lot easier now—that bulk tank means I don't have to cool down that whole room and I don't have to lift those milk cans.

"The next step," he said, "is running a pipe directly from the milking machine to the bulk tank. But I haven't taken that step, and probably won't. It's not all that much problem to carry the milk up and pour it into the bulk tank. That's why I start one side several minutes before the other. If I time it right, when I get back and get the milking machine hooked up on the west side, the east side cow is done. So, once I get started, I'm either running up to the bulk tank or hooking up a milker. You don't want the milking machine to stay on too long—it causes mastitis. I always try to take out the last bit by hand."

Sure enough, for the next hour, Leron was in constant motion: carrying the milker's bucket to the bulk tank, washing down the udders and hooking up the belt and milking machine, running the other side's bucket to the bulk tank, stripping out the last few streams of milk from each teat. Finally, after an hour or so, the cows were finished eating, and Leron was done with the milking.

"Now, we'll check on the calves. Sometimes, the mama cow don't want them and I have to feed them from a bucket. Cows aren't as bad as sheep at rejecting their young, but every now and then, they'll butt the calf away and the poor little feller gets hungry in addition to not at all understanding that he just turned into an orphan."

The calves and the mama cows, however, seemed contented. No rejections, no orphans.

Leron explained that the milk given by the cow for a few days after the calf was born was thick and yellow. "It's called colostrum, and I guess it's full of proteins. It also seems to help the calf fend off diseases. You hardly ever get a sick calf while it's on Mama's milk."

Leron then fed the hogs that had been cooled off by the rain. The storm had moved off to the east while the milking had occurred. As they grunted happily over the ears of corn from the adjacent corn crib, Leron went over and unlatched the gate to the chicken house.

"You notice that the chicken house is on runners, like a big sled. Every week or two, I move it around the pasture, and move the fencing along with it. I don't suppose that the fence would be necessary if it weren't for the road. These chickens seem to be drawn to the gravel, and they don't quite understand about cars. I feed the chickens some cracked corn, but they don't eat much of it. For three seasons they mostly live off weed seeds and bugs."

The chicken house was ever so slightly tipped to one side, and the reason for this soon became clear: The eggs, laid in the wooden nests on the inside of the structure, rolled into the wire mesh cage on the outside of the building. All Leron had to do to gather the eggs was walk along the mesh with a large bucket and collect the eggs.

"I got about a hundred chickens here. They lay way more eggs than we could ever eat, so for a few days I ran an ad in the paper about eggs from free-range chickens, and now I supply about twenty families. They come out here and pick up the eggs on Saturday or Sunday. We get some frying chickens, too, when some of these eggs get hatched out by some of these settin' hens."

This is how a truly free-range egg-laying operation functions. The chickens use the laying house only for egg-laying purposes or to escape from predators. There are no lights and no heating, air-conditioning, or ventilation systems. The chickens spend most of their time foraging in the pastures, catching insects and eating the seeds of plants. Their production may not be equal to those of caged or faux-free-range chickens, but the inputs that are so costly to industrial confinement operations cost the sustainable grower nothing. Occasionally the egg-laying and predator-escape building must be moved to a new location in the pasture to enable the chickens to find new sources of feeds. Finally, the sustainable flock is usually small, normally consisting of a hundred laying hens or less, and is part of an overall sustainable system in which the inputs are mostly derived from other resources on the farm.

Grain, cows, pigs, chickens. Leron's farm is based on the traditional models, but he has picked and chosen from what works. He doesn't use draft horses, he doesn't primarily milk his cows by hand, and he doesn't use leeches or poultices of tobacco to treat diseases or sores.

A year or so ago a group of farmers devoted to sustainability toured an organic dairy farm in central Missouri. The farm was entirely self-contained. The dairy family even had their own system for pasteurizing, homogenizing, and bottling, although they used cartons. Since "certified organic" milk means milk produced by dairy cows that have *never* received any type of antibiotics, the question of illness was raised:

"What do you do with a sick cow? If you give the cow some

type of antibiotic, doesn't this render the cow unfit for organic milk?"

The answer from the dairy farmer astonished this group of sustainable farmers:

"We have never had a sick cow. The problem simply hasn't arisen—and we've been doing this for five years."

The farmers went out to view the herd, but it was difficult to see them all at once, since they were spread out across the rolling green hills for which the Green Hills Harvest Farm is named. The nutrient-rich pasture also supported a flock of about one hundred laying hens and was the source for bales of hay. Near the pasture was a cornfield, and the hog lot was adjacent to that. After the corn is picked, the hogs are turned into the field to clean up any missed ears—and add manure to the field for the next crop.

The milk from Green Hills was selling so fast in area supermarkets (although it was also possible to buy it directly at the farm) that the demand far exceeded the supply. In some supermarkets, which took delivery once a week, the milk, cream, and butter from this organic farm would sell out in one day. This was true even though a gallon of milk from this sustainable organic operation was generally priced about one dollar higher than milk from industrial dairies. People were willing to pay more for its superior taste and quality.

This was markedly apparent in the 2 percent milk from this operation that tasted as if it were "whole" milk. The farmer replied that this had to do with a higher content of solids. The amount of water consumed and appetite enhancers fed to cows at industrial dairies means that the milk produced has a much lower content of solids. In essence, the milk from industrial dairies is watered down while still in the cow.

The organic dairy was absolutely spotless, and its milk was Grade A. Inspectors from the Department of Agriculture and Department of Health came by frequently, and the inspections demonstrated that the sanitary procedures were second to none. However, as the farmer noted, "The customer is the reason we keep our place free of germs. While we are organic, it is the personal confidence in our product that is critical to our success. If someone gets sick from drinking our milk, the word gets out, and we'd be ruined. We don't want to do anything that would spoil our relations with people who buy our milk, butter, and cream."

A bit farther north, Terry Spence had inherited a farm from his father, who had inherited it from his father. This third-generation farm is also situated in rolling green hills. Terry has a traditional cow-calf operation and depends mostly upon the natural environment to produce meat for market. His cows are free-range and antibiotic-free. A local USDA/FSIS-certified slaughterhouse kills his steers and those of his like-minded neighbors and packages their products under the Harmony Beef label. The demand for this natural product far exceeds the ability of Terry and his neighbors to supply it, even though the price per pound is much higher than that for feedlot grain-fed beef.

"I don't do anything much with my cows except let them graze around on the hill pastures. It does get pretty intense at calf delivery time; it seems like the calves are bound and determined to get themselves into all sorts of awkward positions to make delivery as difficult as possible for the mama cow. But other than that time—which demands that I spend most of my time with long rubber gloves on to turn the calves or pull them out—the cows and calves are pretty much on their own.

"As I've told many people, sure I raise my calves for slaughter, but I don't torture them in the process."

There are several benefits to this system, not the least of which is economic. The pastures are fertilized by the very cows that are grazing the grasses in the pasture, ensuring that next year's pasture will be productive. There is no expense in paying a feedlot to "finish them out." There are no expenses associated with buying grains or feed additives of antibiotics, hormones, or appetite enhancers. Once the labor-intensive calving process is completed, the cows and calves spend their time in pastures and under shade trees. Eventually, this life ends at the slaughterhouse gate, but until then, the cows and calves are treated with care and respect.

It is difficult to find independent hog farmers since Smithfield, Premium Standard, Seaboard, and the other large corporations captured the markets. Indeed, in many states there are simply no markets for hogs from independent producers— farmers either sign a very one-sided contract with one of these major companies or they don't raise hogs. There are, however, exceptions, such as Niman Ranch, a cooperative headquartered in Marin County, California, which now has operations throughout the country, including ones in Iowa and North Carolina, the two most intensive Big Pig states. The Niman

Ranch farms provide the meats for local restaurants and su-permarkets, as well as at least one major restaurant chain.

Paul Willis's farm near Thornton, Iowa, is the model that Niman Ranch points to as an example of how hogs should be grown. Animal psychologists long ago discovered that pigs are intelligent and gregarious animals. Sows can be aggressive de-fenders of their young. Paul Willis and other Niman Ranch hog farmers are cognizant of these characteristics and provide the sow and her piglets with the environment and the tools to, in Paul's words, "let a pig be a pig." Paul raises hogs mostly out-side but does provide "hoop houses," nothing more than miniature Quonset huts, for the sows and their litters and for escape from the elements. The sows also have access to straw bedding, which they use both for insulation and to make a "bed" for the piglets.

The hoop houses are located in a large pasture surrounded by a short electric fence. The hogs defecate in the grasses and thus provide the fertilizer for next year's crop. The hoop houses and their hog occupants are moved to a different field each year, because too much manure in one place is counter-productive. Odor is also kept to a minimum by spreading the wastes out in the grasses and moving the hog lots each year.

Paul Willis's farm focuses on hogs, but his is a fully diversi-fied farm. In addition to hogs, his farm has chickens, goats, pi-geons, even fish, and Paul also raises the usual Iowa corn and soybean crops. Each of these is dependent on the others. The animals provide the manure needed as fertilizer to grow the grains, the grains are fed to the animals, and the excess of everything is sold. The circle of sustainability is complete.

Niman Ranch and other such cooperatives guarantee their

producers a price per pound well above the market rate. One such cooperative buys hogs at forty cents above market prices, ensuring that sustainable hog farmers get top dollar for their superior products.

Given the success of many "real farmers," it is no accident or coincidence that the large agribusiness industries tried to amend organic certification rules to allow some of their definitely nonorganic practices to be certified as "organic." There was such an outcry that the USDA had to give in and rewrite the proposed organic standards by removing the offending sections. The secretary of agriculture stated that there were more comments received on the proposed organic standards than any other rule-making proposal by the USDA. The offending sections would have allowed irradiation of food products, application of human municipal sludge containing all sorts of nasty things to otherwise organic crops, and using livestock feeds that contained heavy metals and other dubious ingredients.

Having failed at taking over the organic standards, the industry, with the assistance of Rep. Nathan Deal, R-GA, tacked an amendment onto a totally unrelated bill having to do with Iraq and military spending that would have allowed nonorganic poultry feeds to be substituted for organic feeds when the latter was unavailable and the products still be certified as "organic." Representative Deal admitted that this was done at the request of a large poultry operation in his district. While initially passing both the House and Senate, this measure was repealed due to massive public protests to Congress.

Likewise, egg-laying companies such as Rose Acre Farms are attempting to cash in on the demand for eggs from free-range chickens. In midwestern supermarkets, Rose Acre offers eggs from "free-roaming" chickens, but what Rose Acre means and what the public understands are two completely different matters. The Rose Acre chickens do not roam free on grass and pasturelands but roam entirely within the confines of a huge building, along with several thousand other laying hens. In the minds of Rose Acre's public relations or marketing gurus, free-roam means simply that the hens are not confined in cages. Unfortunately for Rose Acre, this sort of "free-roam" system is not sustainable. There are simply too many inputs. The materials fed to the chickens must be trucked or transported in from a variety of sources: grains from Iowa or Illinois, appetite enhancers from chemical suppliers in New York City, and antibiotics from drug manufacturers everywhere. The building must be ventilated to remove a buildup of toxic fumes from the excrement, and air-conditioning is desirable in the summer and heating necessary in the winter. Lighting is artificial and the bulbs are kept on twenty-four hours per day. The electricity for all this is provided by a utility company, which in itself is unsustainable, using a finite supply of gas, oil, or coal or, even more short-term, generators driven by hydrology through massive dams constructed to create soon-to-be-silted reservoirs.

Don't be duped. It is up to us to ensure that the meat we eat is safe, healthful, and healthy and that the environment, the local economy, family farmers, and workers are protected from the inherent evils of corporate agribusiness. It is time to give production of meat, milk, and eggs back to farmers and small processing plants that care about quality, safety, and tastiness. Buying locally from sustainable producers impacts corporate agribusiness more effectively than any raid or attack on their production and slaughter facilities. An ad hoc boycott of their products will, eventually, bring the entire industry to its knees. It won't happen overnight, next year, or even in the next decade, but as sustainable farming is nurtured with our dollars, the meat we eat will become safe and healthy.

# NOTES

## Sources

The information in this book, as summarized in these notes, came from a variety of sources. I have traveled throughout this country, from the East to West coasts, and have assisted in efforts by local farmers and ranchers to keep out agribusinesses' livestock operations and in these travels have met up with hundreds of people committed to producing what Wendell Berry calls good food.

You have met some of these people in this book, and I have attempted to tell their stories by letting them do the talking. Some are doing well, having found markets for their good foods. Others are barely hanging on. Still others have given up and have left the farm. Finally, there are those who followed the advice of the USDA and university extension agents and "got big." They didn't get big and stay in; they got big and were bankrupted. The farm crisis of the mid-1980s was based on banks' willingness to invest in bigness, with farmland as collateral. The price per acre was devalued, and farmers, banks, and farm supply and equipment stores went bust.

For further reading about farms and farming, try the works of A. V. Krebs, Wes Jackson, Gene Logsdon, Jim Hightower, and Wendell Berry. Hightower and Krebs have been at this a long time; one of their earlier works is listed in the bibliography. Prof. John Ikerd's writings have been an inspiration for me and many others; John is a now-retired rural economist but is a stalwart in the sustainable agriculture movement, believing that agribusiness is trying to use failed industrial techniques "in a post-industrial age."

Information on the poultry companies was taken from their literature and Web sites. The information in the appendixes on the leading companies in each sector was compiled from the industry periodicals or from major agriculture magazines. The information on farm markets comes from the USDA.

Several organizations have compiled much information on corporate agribusiness, and this is available on the following Web sites: Global Resource Action Center for the Environment (GRACE), Sierra Club, and in particular the "Rap Sheet" now updated by GRACE, Natural Resources Defense Council (NRDC), Families Against Rural Messes (FARM), Concerned Citizens for Clean Water, Community Association for Restoration of the Environment (CARE), Farmed and Dangerous, Public Interest Research Group (PIRG), Physicians for Social Responsibility, Keep Antibiotics Working (KAW), and Center for Science in the Public Interest (CSPI). This is just a sampling; each of these sites has links to other sites of interest.

# Preface

This section was written in response to the news that a "downer cow" had tested positive for BSE in a Washington State slaughterhouse. There is much on this issue in the book by Sheldon Rampton and John Stauber (see bibliography), *Mad Cow, USA*. The news outlets in the Pacific Northwest have provided extensive coverage beginning on December 23, 2003—the date of the announcement by the USDA. In particular, the Portland *Oregonian* and the *Seattle Post-Intelligencer* have devoted much attention to the incident. Finally, there is much information available from the few scientists conducting research on BSE/vCJD, and this is available on the Web sites www.prions.org and www.mad-cow.org and the CDC Web site (www.cdc.gov).

# Introduction: Get Big or Get Out

This is a wide-ranging chapter, and much information is from my personal experience in my travels around the country and personal correspondence from those I have met. Specific information comes from the USDA, articles in the *New York Times, Mother Jones, High Country News,* Jean Hager-baumer's "CAFO Notes," legal cases (such as *Ivey v. Gold Kist, Inc.*), the Union of Concerned Scientists, and the Web sites of agribusiness industries. Information about the Greeley/ConAgra recall is gleaned from the *Denver Post* and the *Rocky Mountain News.* The peccadilloes of agribusinesses have been reported on extensively from coast to coast.

I met up with "Juan" in the bus station in Bethany, Missouri, in May of 2002, and we engaged in the conversation (he in broken English, me in pathetic Spanish) reported on in the section titled "An Alien View." In addition to the books (see bibliography) *In the Absence of the Sacred,* by Jerry Mander, and *When Corporations Rule the World,* by David Korten, files of various state and federal agencies were reviewed in documenting the wrong-doings of major agribusiness corporations. Finally, Dianne Halverson, of the Animal Welfare Institute, directed and produced the excellent *And on This Farm* video demonstrating what happens when a large agribusiness industry (in this instance, Premium Standard Farms, which is owned by ContiGroup) moves into a close-knit rural community.

# Big Pig

Much of my experience in helping rural communities keep out large livestock facilities involved hog operations. Thus much of the information in this chapter was taken from direct contact and discussions with Lynn and Jerry McKinley, Rolf and Ilsa Christen, and Clarence and Marilyn Yanke, among others. Specific information on economics, state and federal agencies, and the techniques and methodologies used by large hog operations comes from reports, releases, communications, and articles produced by those engaged in CAFOs. Iowa State University has long been involved in studying the economics of the industrial methods, the U.S. EPA and state equivalents have in place laws and regulations governing CAFOs, and periodicals ranging from general farming magazines such as *Successful Farming* to very species-specific publications such as *National Hog Farmer* provided the perspectives of the hog industry. Again, the Web site of the USDA was very helpful (www.usda.com). The impact of large hog farms on rural communities has been the subject of media reports from Bangor, Maine, to San Diego, California, and from Miami, Florida, to Seattle, Washington.

## Big Chicken and Big Egg

There is a plethora of information on raising broilers and on egg-laying operations, and consequently some effort was expended in separating fact from fiction. The companies involved (see appendix A) all have their perspectives, which are detailed in their literature and Web sites. The Poultry Justice Alliance has been formed of poultry contract growers; their perspective is obviously quite different than the companies, and this, too, is detailed. The Web site of the CDC (www.cdc.gov) was very helpful in documenting the bacteria present in chickens and eggs and the resulting outbreaks of human diseases.

But, as with other portions of this book, the best information came from those individuals directly involved, from the ex-politician, to those struggling to make it in an abusive system, to the reporter who discovered the scene described in this chapter. Various lawsuits have been filed and the courts have ruled (*Buntin v. Perdue Farms; Burger v. Cagle's Farms; Sierra Club v. Tyson,* among many, many others)—those cases have been examined. Finally, the issues of the abuse of migrants workers, environmental pollution, contract growers, and contract language have been covered extensively in the *Arkansas Democrat-Gazette,* the *Cincinnati Enquirer*, the *Tulsa World,* the *Northwest Arkansas News*, and wire stories of the Associated Press.

## Big Milk

As with other chapters of this book, much information was derived from direct contact and communication with those quoted: Len Miracle, among many others. These folks are rural residents who became reluctant neighbors to thousands of dairy cows. In addition to personal contacts, media outlets have also reported extensively on the impacts of huge dairy operations. Articles have appeared in the Twin Falls, Idaho, *Times-News,* the *Amarillo Globe News,* the *Seattle Post-Intelligencer,* and the *Los Angeles Times* and TV reports have been shown on various stations in Boise, Seattle, Portland, Oregon, and Albuquerque.

The Web sites of the USDA, CDC, and California Water Quality Board provided much information for this chapter, as did the Web site of NotMilk (www.notmilk.org). To complement the often dry academic or governmental reports, I paid a visit to large industrial dairy operations in Idaho and to a commercial, but considerably smaller, organic dairy in Missouri. As cited earlier (see notes on the preface), the discovery of a downer dairy cow with BSE triggered many articles and reports in the media of the Pacific Northwest, which in turn led me to contact knowledgeable veterinarians and affected farmers (ones living near Mabton, Washington, the site of the "mad cow").

## Big Beef

In this chapter, much of the focus is on the killing and disassembly of large animals and the results of the emphases on efficiency and speed. In addition to discussions with slaughterhouse workers, I am much indebted to the work of Gail Eisnitz as documented in her book (see bibliography) *Slaughterhouse.* While this book is somewhat painful to read—in that the inhumane treatment of doomed animals is detailed—it provides a startling look inside a slaughterhouse. For a more academic view of the effects of large slaughterhouses on small communities, Don Stull and his colleagues Michael Broadway and David Griffith have edited the book (see bibliography) *Any Way*

*You Cut It.* And the USDA, FSIS, CDC, and FDA Web sites provide much information on sanitation, safety, and diseases. As previously noted, the outbreak caused by contaminated meats from the ConAgra slaughterhouse in Greeley, Colorado, was reported on extensively by the *Denver Post* and *Rocky Mountain News.*

## Big Fish

Much of this chapter was taken from personal communications with members of First Nation, specifically Brian Wadhams, and from correspondence with the organizations the Georgia Strait Alliance and Farmed and Dangerous. Especially helpful were the Web sites of the U.S. Fish and Wildlife Service, the Marine Institute, the British Columbia Ministry of Agriculture, Food and Fisheries, and the companies that own the salmon-rearing pens. The elevated presence of PCBs in pen-raised salmon has been raised by various health organizations and has been covered in a July 30, 2003, article in the *New York Times.* Information on the corporations involved (see appendix A) in the raising of salmon in pens may be found on Web sites of various industry organizations.

## Conclusion: Stay Small and Stay Alive

It was a delight to obtain the information on sustainable agriculture contained in this chapter. Visits to these farms invariably resulted in consumption of vast quantities of pie, cookies, and strong coffee. Much of the information in this chapter stems from kitchen table discussions and personal communications thereafter.

# SELECTED BIBLIOGRAPHY

*Air Pollution from Agricultural Operations*. Proceedings of the Second International Conference, American Society of Agricultural Engineers, 2000.

Berry, Wendell. *The Unsettling of America*. Sierra Club Books, 1996 (first published in 1979). Other books by Wendell Berry include the nonfiction works *The Gift of Good Land, What Are People For?*, and *Another Turn of the Crank* and fiction works *The Long-legged House, The Memory of Old Jack*, and *Jaber Crow*.

Cohen, Robert. *Milk, the Deadly Poison*. Argus Publishing, 1997.

Eisnitz, Gail. *Slaughterhouse*. Prometheus Books, 1997.

Hightower, Jim, and A. V. Krebs. *Hard Tomatoes Hard Times*. Agribusiness Accountability Project, 1972.

Korten, David. *When Corporations Rule the World*. Kumarian Press, 1995.

Mander, Jerry. *In the Absence of the Sacred*. Sierra Club Books, 1991.

Rampton, Sheldon, and John Stauber. *Mad Cow, USA*. Common Courage Press, 1997.

Robinson, Jo. *Why Grassfed Is Best!* Vashon Island Press, 2000.

Shiva, Vandana. *Stolen Harvest: The Hijacking of the Global Food Supply*. South End Press, 1999.

Stull, Donald, Michael Broadway, and David Griffith, eds. *Any Way You Cut It*. University Press of Kansas, 1995.

Thu, Kendall, and E. Paul Durrenberger. *Pigs, Profits and Rural Communities*. State University of New York Press, 1998.

Water Sentinels Campaign (Justin Taylor). *Murky Water, Industrial Dairies and the Failure to Regulate*. Sierra Club Books, 2003.

# APPENDIXES

# APPENDIX A: THE AGRIBUSINESS COMPANIES

## Top Thirty-Nine U.S. Hog Companies—2002
### *Source:* Successful Farming *magazine*

| COMPANY | LOCATIONS |
|---|---|
| 1. Smithfield | VA, NC, UT, MO, OK, IL |
| 2. Premium Standard Farms | MO, NC, TX |
| 3. Seaboard Farms | KS, CO, OK |
| 4. Prestage Farms | NC, MS |
| 5. Cargill | NC, AR, OK |
| 6. Iowa Select | IA |
| 7. Pipestone System | MN, SD, IA, NE, OH |
| 8. Christensen Farms | MN, NE |
| 9. Goldsboro | NC |
| 10. Hanor | OK, NC, WI, IL, OH, IA |
| 11. Tyson | AR, MO, OK (No longer engaged in pork production.) |
| 12. Land O' Lakes | IA, IL, IN, OK, MO, GA |
| 13. Bell/Hormel | CO, ND, NE, MN, IA |
| 14. Heartland Pork | IA, IN, IL |
| 15. Sand System | NE |
| 16. Progressive Swine Technologies | NE |
| 17. Farmland Industries | KS, IA, MN, OK (Went out of business.) |
| 18. Maschoff Pork | IL |
| 19. AMVC Management Service | IA |

| | | |
|---|---|---|
| 20. | Pork Technologies | IA, MN |
| 21. | DeCoster of Iowa | IA |
| 22. | Hatfield-Wenger-Purina | PA |
| 23. | Holden Farms | MN |
| 24. | Texas Farm | TX |
| 25. | Wakefield Pork | MN |
| 26. | Alliance Farms | IL, CO |
| 27. | New Fashion Pork | MN |
| 28. | Clougherty Packing Co. | AZ, CA, WY |
| 29. | TriOak Foods | IA, IL |
| 30. | Coharie Farms | NC |
| 31. | Vall | OK |
| 32. | Schwartz Farms | MN |
| 33. | Swine Graphics Enterprises | IA |
| 34. | Hog Slat | NC |
| 35. | Triple Edge Pork | IL, MO |
| 36. | JC Howard Farms | NC |
| 37. | Gold Kist | GA, AL |
| 38. | Garland Farm Supply | NC, SC, GA |
| 39. | Hitch Pork Producers | OK |

## Top Forty-Two U.S. Broiler Companies
### (rankings by production, March 2003)
*Source:* Successful Farming *magazine*

1. Tyson Foods, Inc.
2. Gold Kist, Inc.
3. Pilgrim's Pride, Inc.
4. ConAgra Poultry Companies
5. Perdue Farms
6. Wayne Farms (owned by ContiGroup Companies)
7. Sanderson Farms, Inc.
8. Cagle's, Inc.
9. Foster Farms

10. Mountaire Farms, Inc.
11. O.K. Foods, Inc.
12. George's, Inc.
13. Fieldale Farms, Inc.
14. Peco Foods, Inc.
15. House of Raeford, Inc.
16. Choctaw Maid Farms, Inc.
17. Townsends, Inc.
18. Allen Family Foods, Inc.
19. Simmons Foods, Inc.
20. Case Foods, Inc.
21. Marshall Durbin Companies
22. Koch Foods, Inc.
23. Mar-Jac, Inc.
24. B. C. Rogers, Inc.
25. Claxton Poultry Farms, Inc.
26. Gold'n Plump Poultry, Inc.
27. Peterson Farms, Inc.
28. Sylvest Farms, Inc.
29. Amick Farms, Inc.
30. Golden-Rod Broilers, Inc.
31. Harrison Poultry, Inc.
32. Charoen Pokphand USA, Inc.
33. Farmers Pride, Inc.
34. Draper Valley Farms, Inc.
35. Empire Kosher Poultry, Inc.
36. Holmes Foods
37. Pennfield Farms
38. Park Farms, Inc.
39. Lady Forest Farms
40. Gentry Poultry Co., Inc.
41. MBA Poultry, LLC
42. College Hill Poultry, Inc.

## Top Sixty U.S. Egg Companies
*Source:* Egg Industry *magazine, January 2003*

| COMPANY | LOCATION OF COMPANY HEADQUARTERS |
|---|---|
| 1. Cal-Maine Foods, Inc. | Jackson, MS |
| 2. Rose Acre Farms | Seymour, IN |
| 3. Michael Foods | Minneapolis, MN |
| 4. Buckeye Egg Farm | Croton, OH |
| 5. DeCoster Egg Farms | Turner, ME |
| 6. Sparboe Farms | Litchfield, MN |
| 7. MOARK Productions | Neosho, MO |
| 8. Dutchland Farms | Lancaster, PA |
| 9. Fort Recovery Equity | Fort Recovery, OH |
| 10. ISE America | Newberry, SC |
| 11. Daybreak Foods | Lake Mills, WI |
| 12. Hillandale Farms | Lake City, FL |
| 13. Golden Oval Eggs | Renville, MN |
| 14. Midwest Poultry | Mentone, IN |
| 15. Wabash Valley Produce | Dubois, IN |
| 16. National Food | Seattle, WA |
| 17. Mahard Egg Farms | Prosper, TX |
| 18. Weaver Bros. | Versailles, OH |
| 19. Maxim Egg Farm | Boling, TX |
| 20. Valley Fresh Foods | Turlock, CA |
| 21. Crystal Farms | Chestnut, GA |
| 22. Tampa Farm Service | Dover, FL |
| 23. Fremont Farms of Iowa | Oskaloosa, IA |
| 24. Daylay Egg Farm, Inc. | West Mansfield, OH |
| 25. Kofkoff Egg Farms | Fitchville, CT |
| 26. Sonstegard Foods | Sioux Falls, SD |
| 27. Creighton Brothers | Warsaw, IN |
| 28. Herbruck Poultry Ranch | Saranac, MI |
| 29. Hickman's Egg Ranch | Glendale, AZ |
| 30. Zephyr Egg | Zephyrhills, FL |

31. Ebenshade Farms | Mount Joy, PA
32. Pilgrim's Pride | Pittsburg, TX
33. Red Bird Farm | Bear, DE
34. Gemperle Enterprise | Turlock, CA
35. Kreider Farms | Manheim, PA
36. McAnally Ranch | Yucaipa, CA
37. Dixie Egg Company | Jacksonville, FL
38. S & R Egg Farms | Whitewater, WI
39. Cooper Farms | Oakwood, OH
40. Hamilton Farm Bureau | Hamilton, MI
41. Hemmelgam & Sons | Coldwater, OH
42. J. S. West Milling Co. | Modesto, CA
43. Delta Egg Farm | Delta, UT
44. Sunrise Acres | Hudsonville, MI
45. Braswell Milling | Nashville, NC
46. Wilcox Farms | Roy, WA
47. Willamette Egg Farms | Canby, OR
48. Sunbest Farms of Iowa | Papetti Farms, Clearfield, IA
49. George's Commercial Egg | Siloam Springs, AR
50. Morning Fresh Farms | Platteville, CO
51. Primera Foods Corp. | Creekwood Farm, Cameron, WI
52. SKS Enterprise | Manteca, CA
53. Lathem Farms | Pendergrass, CA
54. Hoover Egg Co. | Yucaipa, CA
55. Ritewood Egg Farms | Franklin, MO
56. County Charm Egg Dist. | Gainsville, GA
57. Demler Egg Ranch | San Jacinto, CA
58. Feather Crest Farms | Kurten, TX
59. Pine Hill Egg Ranch | Ramona, CA
60. Radlo Bros. | Watertown, ME

# Top Twenty U.S. Milk Producers
## (6,500 to 12,000 cows)
*Source: American Dairy Association*

1. Progressive Dairies, Bakersfield, CA
2. Joseph Gallo Farms, Atwater, CA
3. Hettinga Dairies, Corona, CA
4. Braum's Dairy Farm, Tuttle, OK
5. Larson Dairy, Okeechobee, FL
6. Las Uvas Dairy, Hatch, NM
7. Rockview Dairy, Downey, CA
8. Bos/Bouma Partners, El Paso, TX
9. Arie de Jong, Gilbert, AZ
10. Den Dulk Enterprises, Ravenna, MI
11. Aurora Dairy, Longmont, CO
12. Luis Bettencourt, Jerome, ID
13. McArthur Farms, Okeechobee, FL
14. Syracuse/Timeline, Syracuse, KS
15. Knevelbaard Farms, Corona, CA
16. Case Van der Eyk Jr., Ontario and Tipton, CA
17. Shamrock Farms, Chandler, AZ
18. Alliance Dairies, Trenton, FL
19. Aardema Dairies, Jerome, ID
20. John Reitsma, Jerome, ID

# Top Thirty U.S. Cattle Feedlots
## (As of the fourth quarter of 1999. No up-to-date information is available.)

## *Source:* Cattle Buyers Weekly

1. Cactus Feeders, Inc., Amarillo, TX
2. ContiGroup Cattle Feeding Division, Boulder, CO
3. ConAgra Cattle Feeding Co., Greeley, CO (sold by ConAgra in 2002)

4. Caprock Industries, Amarillo, TX
5. National Farms, Inc., Kansas City, MO
6. J. R. Simplot Company, Boise, ID
7. Cattlco/Liberal Feeders, Memphis, TN
8. Friona Industries L.P., Amarillo, TX
9. Agri-Beef Company, Boise, ID
10. AzTx Cattle Company, Hereford, TX
11. Irsik & Doll, Cimarron, KS
12. Hitch Enterprises, Inc., Guymon, OK
13. Four States Feedyards, Lamar, CO
14. Barrett Crofoot, Inc., Hereford, TX
15. Gottschalk Feeding Corporation, Elkhorn, NE
16. Dinklage Feedyards, Inc., Sidney, NE
17. Harris Feeding Company, Coalinga, CA
18. Pratt Feeders, Inc., Pratt, KS
19. Brookover Companies, Garden City, KS
20. Cattle Empire LLC., Satanta, KS
21. McElhaney Cattle Company, Wellton, AZ
22. Adams Land & Cattle Company, Broken Bow, NE
23. Pinal Feeding Company, Goodyear, AZ
24. Bar-G Feedyard, Hereford, TX
25. Timmerman & Sons Feeding Co., Springfield, NE
26. Bartlett Cattle Company, Kansas City, MO
27. Texas Beef Group, Amarillo, TX
28. Brandt Company, Brawley, CA
29. Bovina Feeders, Farwell, TX
30. Foxley Cattle Company, La Jolla, CA

Top Thirty U.S. Beef Slaughterhouses/Packing Companies
(As of the fourth quarter of 1999.
No up-to-date information is available.)
*Source:* Cattle Buyers Weekly

1. IBP, Inc.
2. ConAgra (sold in 2002)
3. Excel
4. Farmland (sold in 2004)
5. Packerland
6. Nebraska Beef
7. Rosen's
8. Greater Omaha
9. Moyer
10. Taylor
11. American Foods
12. Emmpak Foods
13. Sam Kane
14. L & H
15. Shapiro
16. Beef Packers
17. Washington Beef
18. GFI America
19. Valley Pride
20. Harris Ranch
21. Caviness
22. Lone Star
23. PM Holdings
24. Shamrock Meats
25. Supreme
26. Central Valley
27. San Angelo
28. Aurora
29. Brown
30. Martin's Abattoir

# Top Thirty Global Aquaculture (Salmon) Companies
## (based on tons of production)
### Source: *Aquaculture Magazine Online*

1. Nutreco Holding N.V.
2. Pan Fish ASA
3. Stolt Sea Farm S.A.
4. Fjord Seafood ASA
5. Statkorn Holding ASA
6. Salmones Pacifico Sur S.A.
7. George Weston Ltd.
8. Midnor Group AS
9. Camanchaca S.A.
10. Multiexport S.A.
11. Dårfjord Lake AS
12. Laschinger Holding
13. Salmones Unimarc S.A.
14. Hydrotech Gruppen
15. SalMar AS
16. Hydro Seafood GSP
17. Follalaks Holding AS
18. Trusal S.A.
19. Invertec
20. Cultivos Marinos Chiloé
21. Aguas Claras S.A.
22. Salmones Antartica S.A.
23. Sjøtroll AS
24. Seafarm Invest AS
25. Los Fiordos
26. Vestlax
27. Fjordlaks Aqua AS
28. Pesca Chile
29. Eicosal
30. Bremnes Fryseri

# APPENDIX B: RESOURCES

This is a guide to sustainable producers of meat, milk, and eggs in your area. Ask for the farmers' market nearest you and the name/address/phone number of the local organizer. While in some states it may not be legal to sell meat or animal products at farmers' markets, the local organizer should be able to provide you with the contact information for local producers.

NOTE: The number in parentheses after each state indicates the total number of farmers' markets in that state.

### Alabama (13)

State Farmers' Market Representative George Parris
Alabama Department of Agriculture
1445 Federal Drive
Montgomery, AL 36107
Phone: (334) 240-7250
Fax: (334) 240-7270
E-mail: aada@agi.state.al.us

### Alaska (8)

State Farmers' Market Representative Doug Warner
Alaska Department of Agriculture
1800 Glenn Highway, Suite 12
Palmer, AK 99645
Phone: (907) 745-7200
Fax: (907) 745-7254
E-mail: Douglas_Warner@dnr.state.ak.us

### Arizona (31)

State Farmers' Market Representative Mary Kay Martin
Arizona Department of Agriculture
National Marketing Specialist & Arizona Grown Program
1688 West Adams Street
Phoenix, AZ 85007
Phone: (602) 542-0978

### Arkansas (28)

State Farmers' Market Representative Janet Carson
Arkansas State Plant Board
P.O. Box 391
Little Rock, AR 72203
Phone: (501) 671-2174
E-mail: jcarson@uaex.edu

### California (365)

State Farmers' Market Representative Randii MacNear
California Federation of Certified Farmers Markets
P.O. Box 1813
Davis, CA 95617
Phone: (530) 756-1695
Fax: (530) 756-1858
E-mail: rmacnear@wheel.dcn.davis.ca.us
Web site: http://farmersmarket.ucdavis.edu

## Colorado (47)

State Farmers' Market Representative Loretta Lopez
Colorado Department of Agriculture
Markets Division
700 Kipling Street, Suite 4000
Lakewood, CO 80215
Phone: (303) 239-4115
E-mail: Loretta.Lopez@ag.state.co.us

## Connecticut (64)

State Farmers' Market Representative Rick Macsuga
Connecticut Department of Agriculture
765 Asylum Avenue
Hartford, CT 06105
Phone: (860) 713-2544
Fax: (860) 713-2516

## Delware (2)

State Farmers' Market Representative Melanie Rapp
Delaware Department of Agriculture
2320 South Dupont Highway
Dover, DE 19901
Phone: (302) 739-4811
Fax: (302) 697-6287

## District of Columbia (25)

State Farmers' Market Representative Ann Harvey Yonkers
District of Columbia
American Farmland Trust
1200 18th Street, NW, Suite 800
Washington, DC 20036
Phone: (202) 331-7300 (ext. 3051)
Fax: (202) 659-8339
E-mail: ayonkers@farmland.org

### Florida (63)

State Farmers' Market Representative Tony Young
Florida Department of Agriculture
Bureau of State Markets
407 South Calhoun Street, Suite 209
Tallahassee, FL 32399
Phone: (850) 487-4322
Fax: (850) 488-9006
E-mail: youngr@doacs.state.fl.us

### Georgia (9)

State Farmers' Market Representive Bob Meyer
Georgia Department of Agriculture
19 MLK Jr. Drive
Agriculture Building, Room 324
Atlanta, GA 30334
Phone: (404) 656-3680
Fax: (404) 656-9380
E-mail: bmeyer@agr.state.ga.us

### Hawaii (67)

State Farmers' Market Representative Larry Yamoto
Hawaii Department of Agriculture
1428 South King Street
Honolulu, HI 96814
Phone: (808) 973-9591
Fax: (808) 973-9590

### Idaho (19)

State Farmers' Market Representative Mandi Thompson
Idaho Department of Agriculture
Agricultural Marketing and Development
P.O. Box 790
Boise, ID 83701

Phone: (208) 332-8535
Fax: (208) 334-2879
E-mail: mthompson@agri.state.id.us

## Illinois (130)

State Farmers' Market Representative Kent McFarland
Illinois Department of Agriculture
Bureau of Marketing & Promotion
P.O. Box 19281
Springfield, IL 62794
Phone: (217) 524-5960
Fax: (217) 524-6858
E-mail: kmcfarland@agr.state.il.us

## Indiana (67)

State Farmers' Market Representative Jim Julian
Purdue University
Department of Horticulture & Landscape Architecture
1165 Hort Building
West Lafayette, IN 47907
Phone: (765) 494-0797
Fax: (765) 494-0391
E-mail: julian@hort.purdue.edu

## Iowa (141)

State Farmers' Market Representative Barbara Lovitt
Iowa Department of Agriculture
Wallace State Office Building
Des Moines, IA 50319
Phone: (515) 281-8232
Fax: (515) 242-5015
E-mail: barb.lovitt@idals.state.us.ia

### Kansas (67)

State Farmers' Market Representative Karen Gast
Kansas State University
Horticulture, Forestry, & Recreation Resources
2021 Throckmorton Hall
Manhattan, KS 66506
Phone: (785) 532-1439
E-mail: klbg@ksu.edu

### Kentucky (86)

State Farmers' Market Representative Anna Sidebottom
Kentucky Department of Agriculture
100 Fair Oaks Lane, 5th Floor
Frankfort, KY 40601
Phone: (502) 564-0290 ext. 262
Fax: (502) 564-0303
E-mail: Anna.Lucio@kyagr.com

### Louisiana (19)

State Farmers' Market Representative Jimmy Boudreaux
Louisiana Department of Agriculture
155 J.C. Miller Hall
Baton Rouge, LA 70803
Phone: (225) 578-2222
Fax: (225) 578-0773
E-mail: JBoudreaux@agctr.lsu.edu

### Maine (57)

State Farmers' Market Representative Deanne Herman
Maine Department of Agriculture
Marketing & Products Development
28 State House Station
Augusta, ME 04333
Phone: (207) 287-7561

Fax: (207) 287-5576

E-mail: maine.grown@state.me.us

## Maryland (53)

State Farmers' Market Representative Tony Evans

Maryland Department of Agriculture

50 Harry South Truman Parkway

Annapolis, MD 21401

Phone: (410) 841-5770

Fax: (410) 841-5914

## Massachusetts (87)

State Farmers' Market Representative David Webber

Massachusetts Department of Food and Agriculture

251 Causeway Street, Suite 500

Boston, MA 02114

Phone: (617) 626-1700

Fax: (617) 626-1850

E-mail: David.Webber@state.ma.us

## Michigan (66)

State Farmers' Market Representative Susan Smalley

Michigan State University

A270 Plant & Soil Science Building

East Lansing, MI 48824

Phone: (517) 432-0049

Fax: (517) 353-3834

E-mail: smalley@msue.msu.edu

## Minnesota (55)

State Farmers' Market Representative Ruth White

Minnesota Department of Agriculture

Agricultural Marketing & Development

90 West Plato Boulevard

St. Paul, MN 55107

Phone: (657) 297-5794

E-mail: ruth.white@state.mn.us

### Mississippi (18)

State Farmers' Market Representative Billy Carter

Mississippi Department of Agriculture

P.O. Box 4629

Jackson, MS 39296

Phone: (601) 354-6573

Fax: (601) 354-7330

E-mail: Billy@mdax.state.ms.us

### Missouri (102)

State Farmers' Market Representative Tammy Bruckerhoff

Missouri Department of Agriculture

P.O. Box 630

Jefferson City, MO 65102

Phone: (573) 751-3394

Fax: (573) 751-2868

E-mail: Tammy_Bruckerhoff@mail.mda.state.mo.us

### Montana (17)

State Farmers' Market Representative Angelyn Stonebraker

Montana Department of Agriculture

P.O. Box 200201

Helena, MT 59620

Phone: (406) 444-2402

Fax: (406) 444-9442

E-mail: astonebraker@state.mt.us

### Nebraska (39)

State Farmers' Market Representative Dan Korber

Nebraska Department of Agriculture

P.O. Box 94947

Lincoln, NE 68509

Phone: (800) 422-6692

Fax: (402) 471-4876

E-mail: danielak@agr.state.ne.us

## Nevada (16)

State Farmers' Market Representative Peggy McKie

Nevada Division of Agriculture

350 Capitol Hill Avenue

Reno, NV 89502

Phone: (775) 688-1182, ext. 246

Fax: (775) 688-1178

E-mail: pgmckie@govmail.state.nv.us

## New Hampshire (30)

State Farmers' Market Representative Gail McWilliam

New Hampshire Department of Agriculture Markets & Food

P.O. Box 2042

Concord, NH 03302

Phone: (603) 271-3788

Fax: (603) 271-1109

E-mail: gmwilliam@compuserve.com

## New Jersey (47)

State Farmers' Market Representative Ronald Good

New Jersey Department of Agriculture

P.O. Box 330

Trenton, NJ 08625

Phone: (609) 292-8853

E-mail: ron.good@ag.state.nj.us

## New Mexico (36)

State Farmers' Market Representative Craig Mapel

New Mexico Department of Agriculture

P.O. Box 637
Alcalde, NM 87511
Phone: (505) 852-3088
Fax: (505) 852-3088
E-mail: cmapel@la-tierra.com

### New York (268)

State Farmers' Market Representative Robert Lewis
New York Department of Agriculture & Markets
55 Hanson Place
Brooklyn, NY 11217
Phone: (718) 722-2830
Fax: (718) 722-2836
E-mail: Bob.Lewis@agmkt.state.ny.us

### North Carolina (84)

State Farmers' Market Representative Ross Williams
North Carolina Department of Agriculture
P.O. Box 27647
Raleigh, NC 27611
Phone: (919) 733-7887
Fax: (919) 715-0155
E-mail: ross.f.williams@ncmail.net

### North Dakota (22)

State Farmers' Market Representative Sara Wagner
North Dakota Department of Agriculture
600 East Boulevard, Dept. 602
Bismarck, ND 58505
Phone: (800) 242-7535
Fax: (701) 328-4567
E-mail: sawagner@state.nd.us

## Ohio (73)

State Farmers' Market Representative Deanne Maus
Ohio Department of Agriculture
8995 East Main Street
Reynoldsburg, OH 43068
Phone: (614) 466-5532
Fax: (614) 644-5017
E-mail: maus@odant.agri.state.oh.us

## Oklahoma (25)

State Farmers' Market Representative Jason Harvey
Oklahoma Department of Agriculture
P.O. Box 528804
Oklahoma City, OK 73152
Phone: (405) 522-5563
Fax: (405) 522-4855
E-mail: joe.okaagri@mail.okag.state.ok.us

## Oregon (58)

State Farmers' Market Representative Laura Barton
Oregon Department of Agriculture
1207 Northwest Naito Parkway, Suite 104
Portland, OR 97204
Phone: (503) 872-6600
Fax: (503) 872-6601

## Pennsylvania (152)

State Farmers' Market Representative Kathy Cutman
Pennsylvania Department of Agriculture
2301 North Cameron Street
Harrisburg, PA 17110
Phone: (717) 787-4210
Fax: (717) 787-1858

### Rhode Island (16)

State Farmers' Market Representative Peter Susi
Rhode Island Department of Agriculture
235 Promenade Street
Providence, RI 02908
Phone: (401) 222-2781
Fax: (401) 222-6047

### South Carolina (35)

State Farmers' Market Representative Robert Mickle
South Carolina Department of Agriculture
P.O. Box 11280
Columbia, SC 29211
Phone: (803) 734-2210
Fax: (803) 734-2192
E-mail: rmickle@scda.state.sc.us

### South Dakota (9)

State Farmers' Market Representative Jon Farris
South Dakota Department of Agriculture
523 East Capital Avenue
Pierre, SD 57501
Phone: (605) 773-5436
Fax: (605) 773-3481
E-mail: jon.farris@state.sd.us

### Tennessee (45)

State Farmers' Market Representative Laura Fortune
Tennessee Department of Agriculture
Market Development Division—Ellington Agricultural Center
P.O. Box 40627
Nashville, TN 37204
Phone: (615) 837-5349
Fax: (615) 837-5194
E-mail: laurafortune@state.tn.us

## Texas (99)

State Farmers' Market Representative Jim Jones
Texas Department of Agriculture
P.O. Box 12847
Austin, TX 78711
Phone: (512) 463-7420
Fax: (512) 463-9968
E-mail: jjones@agr.state.tx.us

## Utah (13)

State Farmers' Market Representative Richard L. Sparks
Utah Department of Agriculture
Division of Marketing & Conservation
P.O. Box 146500
Salt Lake City, UT 84114
Phone: (801) 538-4913
Fax: (801) 538-9436

## Vermont (45)

State Farmers' Market Representative Lindsey Ketchel
Vermont Department of Agriculture, Food & Markets
116 State Street, Drawer 20
Montpelier, VT 05620
Phone: (802) 828-2416
Fax: (802) 828-3631
E-mail: lindsey@agr.state.vt.us

## Virginia (76)

State Farmers' Market Representative Susan Simpson
Virginia Department of Agriculture & Consumer Services
P.O. Box 1163
Richmond, VA 23218
Phone: (804) 786-2112
Fax: (804) 371-7786
E-mail: ssimpson@vdacs.state.va.us

## Washington (77)

State Farmers' Market Representative Zachary Lyons
Washington Department of Agriculture
P.O. Box 30727
Seattle, WA 98103
Phone: (206) 706-5198
E-mail: zach@wafarmersmarkets.com

## West Virginia (24)

State Farmers' Market Representative Jean Smith
West Virginia Department of Agriculture
Marketing & Development Division
1900 Kanawha Boulevard, East
Charleston, WV 25305
Phone: (304) 558-2210
Fax: (304) 558-2270
E-mail: jsmith@ag.state.wv.us

## Wisconsin (149)

State Farmers' Market Representative Kathy Neher
Wisconsin Department of Agriculture
Division of Marketing
P.O. Box 8911
Madison, WI 53708
Phone: (608) 224-5112
Fax: (608) 224-5111

## Wyoming (7)

State Farmers' Market Representative Linda Hollings
Wyoming Department of Agriculture
2219 Carey Avenue
Cheyenne, WY 82002
Phone: (307) 777-6577
Fax: (307) 777-6593
E-mail: lholli@missc.state.wy.us

# APPENDIX C: LAND-GRANT SCHOOLS

- Alabama A&M University
- Alcorn State University
- Auburn University
- Clemson University
- Colorado State University
- Cornell University
- Delaware State College
- Florida A&M University
- Fort Valley State College
- Iowa State University
- Kansas State University
- Kentucky State University
- Langston University
- Lincoln University
- Louisiana State University
- Michigan State University
- Mississippi State University
- New Mexico State University
- North Carolina A&T University
- North Carolina State University
- North Dakota State University

- Ohio State University
- Oklahoma State University
- Oregon State University
- Pennsylvania State University
- Prairie View A&M University
- Purdue University
- South Carolina State University
- South Dakota State University
- Southern University
- Tennessee State University
- Texas A&M University
- Tuskegee University
- University of Alaska—Fairbanks
- University of Arizona
- University of Arkansas
- University of Arkansas—Pine Bluff
- University of California
- University of Connecticut
- University of Delaware
- University of Florida
- University of Georgia
- University of Guam
- University of Hawaii
- University of Idaho
- University of Illinois
- University of Kentucky
- University of Maine
- University of Maryland
- University of Maryland—College Park
- University of Massachusetts
- University of Minnesota
- University of Missouri
- University of Nebraska
- University of Nevada—Reno
- University of New Hampshire
- University of New Jersey
- University of Puerto Rico

- University of Rhode Island
- University of Tennessee
- University of the District of Columbia
- University of the Virgin Islands
- University of Vermont
- University of Wisconsin—Madison
- University of Wyoming
- Utah State University
- Virginia Polytechnic Institute and State University
- Virginia State University
- Washington State University
- West Virginia University

# ACKNOWLEDGMENTS

I WISH TO THANK THOSE PEOPLE MENTIONED IN THIS book—Terry and Linda Spence, Lynn and Jerry McKinley, Rolf and Ilsa Christen, Jack Parrish, Barb Buckmeier, Clarence and Marilyn Yanke, Bill Buck, Brian Wadhams, John Ikerd, Leron Small, Paul Willis, the anonymous folks in southwest Missouri, and the various people in the Magic Valley. My colleagues at the Sierra Club provided invaluable assistance— Scott Dye, Hank Graddy, Aloma Dew, Laura Krebsbach, and others. Thanks also to all of my family and our farm neighbors and friends in western Kentucky, where I was born and raised. Special thanks go to Wendell Berry; if I know anything about good farming and land stewardship, it is due to his works.

Kendra Kimbarauskas, once of Des Moines, Iowa, now in Portland, Oregon, read through the earlier drafts of this book and made many suggestions for change. She stated constantly that I was using "jargon." Hmmmph.

I would be remiss if I failed to thank my literary agent, Sandra Dijkstra, and her staff for shepherding this project through the initial phases. Last, but certainly not least, I thank the ever patient and careful editors at St. Martin's Press, Tim Bent and Julia Pastore.

# INDEX